SAT Vocabulary Prep
Level 2

Other Kaplan Books for College-Bound Students

SAT Vocabulary Prep Level 1
SAT Premier Program
SAT Comprehensive Program
12 Practice Tests for the SAT
SAT Strategies for Super Busy Students
SAT 2400
SAT Critical Reading Workbook
SAT Math Workbook
SAT Writing Workbook
SAT in a Box
Warcraft Vol.1: A Kaplan SAT/ACT Vocabulary-Building Manga
Psy-Comm Vol. 1: A Kaplan SAT/ACT Vocabulary-Building Manga
Van Von Hunter Vol. 1: A Kaplan SAT/ACT Vocabulary-Building Manga
The Ring of McAllister: A Score-Raising Mystery Featuring
1,046 Must-Know SAT Vocabulary Words
Frankenstein: A Kaplan SAT Score-Raising Classic
The Tales of Edgar Allan Poe: A Kaplan SAT Score-Raising Classic
Dr. Jekyll and Mr. Hyde: A Kaplan SAT Score-Raising Classic
Wuthering Heights: A Kaplan SAT Score-Raising Classic
The War of the Worlds: A Kaplan SAT Score-Raising Classic

SAT Vocabulary Prep
Level 2

KAPLAN

PUBLISHING

New York

© 2008 Kaplan, Inc.

Published by Kaplan Publishing, a division of Kaplan, Inc.
1 Liberty Plaza, 24th Floor
New York, NY 10006

Printed in the United States of America

December 2008
10 9 8 7 6 5 4 3 2

ISBN-13: 978-1-4195-5014-0

Kaplan Publishing books are available at special quantity discounts to use for sales promotions, employee premiums, or educational purposes. Please email our Special Sales Department to order or for more information at kaplanpublishing@kaplan.com, or write to Kaplan Publishing, 1 Liberty Plaza, 24th Floor, New York, NY 10006.

HOW TO USE THIS BOOK

Kaplan's *SAT Vocabulary Prep Level 2* is designed to help you learn 500 of the hardest SAT vocabulary words in a quick and easy way.

- There are three vocabulary words on the front of each page (including part of speech and pronunciation). On the back you'll find the definition, a sample sentence with the SAT word in action, and synonyms of the word.

- The vocabulary words in the book are color-coded by level of difficulty to make navigating the book easier and studying more fun.

- As a special bonus, we've included an SAT word root list at the back of this book for extra studying power.

Looking for still more SAT prep? Be sure to pick up a copy of Kaplan's *SAT Vocabulary Prep Level 1*, with 500 additional words that often appear on the SAT.

Good luck!

ABANDON
noun (uh <u>baan</u> duhn)

······································

ABORTIVE
adj (uh <u>bohr</u> tihv)

······································

ABSCOND
verb (aab <u>skahnd</u>)

total lack of inhibition

With her strict parents out of town, Kelly danced all night with **abandon.**

synonyms: exuberance, enthusiasm

• •

ending without results

Her **abortive** attempt to swim the full five miles left her frustrated.

synonyms: fruitless, futile, unsuccessful

• •

to leave quickly in secret

The criminal **absconded** during the night with all of his mother's money.

synonyms: slip, sneak, flee

ACCRETION
noun (uh <u>kree</u> shuhn)

· ·

ACME
noun (<u>aak</u> mee)

· ·

ACTUATE
verb (<u>aak</u> choo ayt)

a growth in size, an increase in amount

The committee's strong fund-raising efforts resulted in an **accretion** in scholarship money.

synonyms: buildup, accumulation

· ,

the highest level or degree attainable

Just when he reached the **acme** of his power, the dictator was overthrown.

synonyms: apex, peak, summit

· ·

to put into motion, to activate; to motivate or influence to activity

The leader's rousing speech **actuated** the crowd into a peaceful protest.

synonyms: incite, instigate

BASIC

ACUITY
noun (uh <u>kyoo</u> ih tee)

· ·

ACUMEN
noun (<u>aak</u> yuh muhn) (uh <u>kyoo</u> muhn)

· ·

ADAMANT
adj (<u>aad</u> uh muhnt) (<u>aad </u>uh mint)

sharp vision or perception characterized by the ability to resolve fine detail

With unusual **acuity**, she was able to determine that the masterpiece was a fake.

synonyms: acuteness, sharpness

• •

sharpness of insight, mind, and understanding; shrewd judgment

The investor's financial **acumen** helped him to select high-yield stocks.

synonyms: discernment, shrewdness

• •

stubbornly unyielding

She was **adamant** about leaving the restaurant after the waiter was rude.

synonyms: inflexible, obdurate, inexorable

BASIC

ADEPT
adj (uh <u>dehpt</u>)

. . . .

ADMONISH
verb (aad <u>mahn</u> ihsh)

. . . .

ADULATION
noun (<u>aaj</u> juh lay shuhn)

BASIC

extremely skilled

She is **adept** at computing math problems in her head.

synonyms: quick, masterful

• •

to caution or warn gently in order to correct something

My mother **admonished** me about my poor grades.

synonyms: berate, rebuke

• •

excessive flattery or admiration

The **adulation** she showed her professor seemed insincere; I suspected she really wanted a better grade.

synonyms: fawning, buttering up

ALGORITHM
verb (<u>aal</u> guh rith uhm)

....

ALLAY
verb (uh <u>lay</u>)

....

AMITY
noun (<u>aa</u> mih tee)

BASIC

an established procedure for solving a problem or equation

The accountant uses a series of **algorithms** to determine the appropriate tax bracket.

synonym: calculation

· ·

to lessen, ease, reduce in intensity

Trying to **allay** their fears, the nurse sat with them all night.

synonyms: alleviate, soothe

· ·

friendship, good will

Correspondence over the years contributed to a lasting **amity** between the women.

synonym: harmony

ANOMALY
noun (uh <u>nahm</u> uh lee)

....

ANTIQUATED
adj (<u>aan</u> tih kway tihd)

....

APLOMB
noun (uh <u>plahm</u>) (uh <u>pluhm</u>)

BASIC

a deviation from the common rule, something that is difficult to classify

Among the top-ten albums of the year was one **anomaly**—a compilation of polka classics.

synonym: irregularity

• •

too old to be fashionable or useful

Next to her coworker's brand-new model, Marisa's computer looked **antiquated**.

synonyms: outdated, obsolete

• •

self-confident assurance; poise

For such a young dancer, she had great **aplomb**, making her perfect to play the young princess.

synonyms: coolness, composure

BASIC

APPRISE
verb (uh <u>priez</u>)

· ·

APPROPRIATE
verb (uh <u>proh</u> pree ayt)

· ·

ARCANE
adj (ahr <u>kayn</u>)

BASIC

to give notice to, inform

"Thanks for **apprising** me that the test time has been changed," said Emanuel.

synonym: notify

· ·

to assign to a particular purpose, allocate

The fund's manager **appropriated** funds for the clean-up effort.

synonyms: appoint, earmark

· ·

secret, obscure; known only to a few

The **arcane** rituals of the sect were passed down through many generations.

synonyms: esoteric, mysterious

ASSENT
verb (uh <u>sehnt</u>)

· ·

AWRY
adv (uh <u>rie</u>)

· ·

BALK
verb (bawk)

BASIC

to agree, as to a proposal

After careful deliberation, the CEO **assented** to the proposed merger.

synonyms: accede, yield, concur

•••

crooked, askew, amiss

Something must have gone **awry** in the computer system because some of my files are missing.

synonyms: aslant, wrong

•••

to stop short and refuse to go on

When the horse **balked** at jumping over the high fence, the rider was thrown off.

synonyms: flinch, shirk from

BEATIFIC
adj (bee uh <u>tihf</u> ihk)

....

BEDRAGGLE
adj (bih <u>draag</u> uhld)

....

BEGET
verb (bih <u>geht</u>)

displaying calmness and joy, relating to a state of celestial happiness

After spending three months in India, she had a **beatific** peace about her.

synonyms: angelic, blissful

• •

soiled, wet and limp; dilapidated

The child's **bedraggled** blanket needed a good cleaning.

synonyms: dishevelled, disordered, threadbare

• •

to produce, especially as an effect or outgrowth; to bring about

The mayor believed that finding petty offenders would help reduce serious crime because, he argued, small crimes **beget** big crimes.

synonyms: cause, breed

BASIC

BEHEMOTH
noun (buh <u>hee</u> muhth)

· ·

BENEFICENT
adj (buh <u>nehf</u> ih sent)

· ·

BERATE
verb (bih <u>rayt</u>)

BASIC

something of monstrous size or power;
huge creature

The budget became such a **behemoth** that
observers believed the film would never make
a profit.

synonyms: giant, mammoth

• •

pertaining to an act of kindness

The **beneficent** man donated the money
anonymously.

synonyms: charitable, generous

• •

to scold harshly

When my manager found out I had handled the
situation so insensitively, he **berated** me.

synonym: criticize

BASIC

BLASPHEMOUS
adj (<u>blaas</u> fuh muhs)

....

BLATANT
adj (<u>blay</u> tnt)

....

BOVINE
adj (<u>boh</u> vien)

cursing, profane; extremely irreverent

The politician's offhanded biblical references seemed **blasphemous,** given the context of the orderly meeting.

synonyms: foul-mouthed

• •

completely obvious and conspicuous, especially in an offensive, crass manner

Such **blatant** advertising within the bounds of the school drew protest from parents.

synonyms: obvious, flagrant

• •

relating to cows; having qualities characteristic of a cow, such as sluggishness or dullness

His **bovine** demeanor did nothing to engage me.

synonyms: dull, placid

BRAGGART
noun (<u>braag</u> uhrt)

· ·

BROACH
verb (brohch)

· ·

CACHE
noun (caash)

BASIC

a person who brags or boasts in a loud and empty manner

Usually the biggest **braggart** at the company party, Susan's boss was unusually quiet at this year's event.

synonyms: boaster, showoff

• •

to mention or suggest for the first time

Sandy wanted to go to college away from home, but he didn't know how to **broach** the topic with his parents.

synonyms: introduce, propose

• •

a hiding place; stockpile

It's good to have a **cache** where you can stash your cash.

synonyms: hoard, reserve

CANTANKEROUS
adj (kaan <u>taang</u> kuhr uhs)

••

CATACLYSMIC
adj (<u>kaat</u> uh <u>klihz</u> mihk)

••

CATALYST
noun (<u>kaat</u> uhl ihst)

having a difficult, uncooperative, or stubborn disposition

The most outwardly **cantankerous** man in the nursing home was surprisingly sweet and loving with his grandchildren.

synonyms: contentious, ornery

. . . .

severely destructive

By all appearances, the storm seemed **cataclysmic,** though it lasted only a short while.

synonyms: catastrophic, tragic

. . . .

something that provokes or speeds up significant change, especially without being affected by the consequences

Technology has been a **catalyst** for the expansion of alternative education, such as home schooling and online courses.

synonym: accelerator

CAUCUS
noun (<u>kaw</u> kuhs)

· ·

CESSATION
noun (seh <u>say</u> shuhn)

· ·

CIRCUMVENT
verb (suhr kuhm <u>vehnt</u>)

BASIC

a closed committee within a political party; a private committee meeting

The president met with the delegated **caucus** to discuss the national crisis.

synonyms: assembly, convention

• •

a temporary or complete halt

The **cessation** of hostilities ensured that soldiers were able to spend the holidays with their families.

synonyms: arrest, termination

• •

to go around; avoid

Laura was able to **circumvent** the hospital's regulations, slipping into her mother's room long after visiting hours were over.

synonyms: evade, sidestep

BASIC

COAGULATE
verb (koh <u>aag</u> yuh layt)

· ·

COLLOQUIAL
adj (kuh <u>loh</u> kwee uhl)

· ·

COMMUTE
verb (kuh <u>myoot</u>)

BASIC

to clot; to cause to thicken

Hemophiliacs can bleed to death from a minor cut because their blood does not **coagulate**.

synonyms: jell, congeal

• •

characteristic of informal speech

The book was written in a **colloquial** style so it would be user-friendlier.

synonyms: conversational, idiomatic

• •

to change a penalty to a less severe one

In exchange for cooperating with detectives on another case, the criminal had his charges **commuted**.

synonyms: exchange, mitigate

COMPLACENT
adj (kuhm <u>play</u> sihnt)

· ·

COMPLIANT
adj (kuhm <u>plie</u> uhnt)

· ·

CONDOLE
verb (kuhn <u>dohl</u>)

BASIC

self-satisfied, smug

Alfred always shows a **complacent** smile whenever he wins the spelling bee.

synonyms: contented, unconcerned

• •

submissive, yielding

The boss was unused to an assistant who spoke her mind, but he grew to respect the fact that she wasn't **compliant**.

synonyms: malleable, complacent, tractable, acquiescent

• •

to grieve; to express sympathy

My hamster died when I was in third grade, and my friends **condoled** with me and helped bury him in the yard.

synonyms: console, sympathize

CONSTERNATION
noun (kahn stuhr <u>nay</u> shuhn)

....

CONSTITUENT
noun (kuhn <u>stih</u> choo uhnt)

....

CONSTRAINT
noun (kuhn <u>straynt</u>)

BASIC

an intense state of fear or dismay

One would never think that a seasoned hunter would display such **consternation** when a grizzly bear lumbered too close to camp.

synonyms: cowardice, fear

....

component, part; citizen, voter

A machine will not function properly if one of its **constituents** is defective.

synonyms: element, factor

....

something that restricts or confines within prescribed bounds

Given the **constraints** of the budget, it was impossible to accomplish my goals.

synonyms: limitation, check

CONTEMPTUOUS
adj (kuhn <u>tehmp</u> choo uhs)

···

CONVALESCE
verb (kahn vuhl <u>ehs</u> uhns)

···

COVERT
adj (koh <u>vuhrt</u>)

scornful; expressing contempt

The diners were intimidated by the waiter's **contemptuous** manner.

synonyms: derisive, disdainful, supercilious

• •

to gradually recover from an illness

After her bout with malaria, Tatiana needed to **convalesce** for a whole month.

synonyms: heal, recuperate

• •

secretive, not openly shown

The **covert** military operation wasn't disclosed until weeks later after it was determined to be a success.

synonym: veiled

CUMULATIVE
adj (<u>kyoom</u> yuh luh tihv)

....

CURT
adj (kuhrt)

....

DEBACLE
noun (dih <u>baa</u> kuhl)

increasing, collective

The new employee didn't mind her job at first, but the daily petty indignities had a **cumulative** demoralizing effect.

synonyms: added up, gradual

• •

abrupt, short with words

The grouchy shop assistant was **curt** with one of her customers, which resulted in a reprimand from her manager.

synonyms: terse, rude

• •

a sudden, disastrous collapse or defeat; a total, ridiculous failure

It was hard for her to show her face in the office after the **debacle** of spilling coffee on her supervisor—three times.

synonyms: crash, wreck

DEFAMATORY
adj (dih <u>faam</u> uh tohr ee)

••

DIFFUSE
verb (dih <u>fyooz</u>)

••

DIGRESS
verb (die <u>grehs</u>)

BASIC

injurious to the reputation

The tabloid was sued for making **defamatory** statements about the celebrity.

synonyms: libelous, slanderous

....

to spread out widely, to scatter freely, to disseminate

They turned on the fan, but all that did was **diffuse** the cigarette smoke throughout the room.

synonyms: disperse, soften

....

to turn aside, especially from the main point; to stray from the subject

The professor repeatedly **digressed** from the topic, boring his students.

synonyms: deviate, wander

DISCRETE
adj (dih <u>skreet</u>)

· ·

ELEGY
noun (<u>eh</u> luh jee)

· ·

ELUDE
verb (ih <u>lood</u>)

BASIC

individually distinct, separate

What's nice about the CD is that each song functions as a **discrete** work and also as part of the whole compilation.

synonyms: unconnected, distinct

· ·

a mournful poem, usually about the dead

A memorable **elegy** was read aloud for the spiritual leader.

synonyms: memorial, lament

· ·

to avoid cleverly, to escape the perception of

Somehow, the runaway **eluded** detection for weeks.

synonyms: evade, dodge

EUTHANASIA
noun (yoo thun <u>nay</u> zhuh)

. . . .

EXPUNGE
verb (ihk <u>spuhnj</u>)

. . . .

FEIGN
verb (fayn)

BASIC

the practice of ending the life of hopelessly ill individuals; assisted suicide

Euthanasia has always been the topic of much moral debate.

synonyms: mercy-killing

· ·

to erase, eliminate completely

The parents' association **expunged** the questionable texts from the children's reading list.

synonyms: delete, obliterate

· ·

to pretend, to give a false appearance of

Though she had discovered they were planning a party, she **feigned** surprise so as not to spoil the festivities.

synonyms: fake

FERAL
adj (<u>fehr</u> uhl)

· ·

FITFUL
adj (<u>fiht</u> fuhl)

· ·

FORGO
verb (fohr <u>goh</u>)

suggestive of a wild beast, not domesticated

Though the animal-rights activists did not want to see the **feral** dogs harmed, they offered no solution to the problem.

synonyms: wild, savage

· ·

intermittent, lacking steadiness; characterized by irregular bursts of activity

Her **fitful** breathing became cause for concern, and eventually, she phoned the doctor.

synonyms: sporadic, periodic

· ·

to do without, to abstain from

As much as I wanted to **forgo** statistics, I knew it would serve me well in my field of study.

synonym: pass on

FORMIDABLE
adj (<u>fohr</u> mih duh buhl)
(fohr <u>mih</u> duh buhl)

....

HIATUS
noun (hie <u>ay</u> tuhs)

....

HYPOCRITE
noun (<u>hih</u> puh kriht)

fearsome, daunting; tending to inspire awe
or wonder

The wrestler was not very big, but his skill and
speed made him a **formidable** opponent.

synonym: overpowering

• •

a gap or interruption in space, time, or continuity

After a long **hiatus** in Greece, the philosophy
professor returned to university.

synonym: break

• •

one who puts on a false appearance of virtue; one
who criticizes a flaw he in fact possesses

What a **hypocrite**: He criticizes those who wear
fur but then he buys for himself a leather
shearling coat.

synonyms: pretender, deceiver

INCANDESCENT
adj (ihn kahn <u>dehs</u> uhnt)

....

INCORRIGIBLE
adj (ihn <u>kohr</u> ih juh buhl)

....

INCREDULOUS
adj (ihn <u>krehj</u> uh luhs)

shining brightly

The **incandescent** glow of the moon made it a night I'll never forget.

synonyms: brilliant, radiant

• •

incapable of being corrected or amended; difficult to control or manage

"You're **incorrigible**," yelled the frustrated mother to her son, in the middle of his third tantrum of the day.

synonyms: delinquent, unfixable

• •

unwilling to accept what is true, skeptical

The Lasky children were **incredulous** when their parents sat them down and told them the facts of life.

synonyms: doubtful, disbelieving

BASIC

INDOMITABLE
adj (ihn <u>dahm</u> ih tuuh buhl)

....

INGRATIATE
verb (ihn <u>gray</u> shee ayt)

....

INSOLENT
adj (<u>ihn</u> suh luhnt)

BASIC

incapable of being conquered

Climbing Mount Everest would seem an **indomitable** task, but it has been done many times.

synonym: insurmountable

• •

to gain favor with another by deliberate effort, to seek to please somebody so as to gain an advantage

The new intern tried to **ingratiate** herself with the managers so that they might consider her for a future job.

synonyms: flatter, curry favor

• •

insultingly arrogant, overbearing

After having spoken with three **insolent** customer service representatives, Shelly was relieved when the fourth one sympathized with her complaint.

synonyms: offensive, rude

INTIMATION
noun (ihn tuh <u>may</u> shuhn)

· ·

IRONIC
adj (ie <u>rahn</u> ihk)

· ·

IRREVERENT
adj (ih <u>rehv</u> uhr uhnt)

BASIC

a subtle and indirect hint

Abby chose to ignore Babu's **intimation** that she wasn't as good a swimmer as she claimed.

synonyms: suggestion, insinuation

· ·

poignantly contrary or incongruous to what was expected

It was **ironic** to learn that shy Wendy from high school grew up to be the loud-mouth host of the daily talk show.

· ·

disrespectful in a gentle or humorous way

Kevin's **irreverent** attitude toward the principal annoyed the teacher but amused the other children.

synonyms: cheeky, satiric

BASIC

JETTISON
verb (<u>jeht</u> ih zuhn) (<u>jeht</u> ih suhn)

. . . .

KISMET
noun (<u>kihz</u> meht) (<u>kihz</u> miht)

. . . .

LAMPOON
verb (laam <u>poon</u>)

BASIC

to discard, to get rid of as unnecessary or encumbering

The sinking ship **jettisoned** its cargo in a desperate attempt to reduce its weight.

synonyms: eject, dump

· ·

fate

When Eve found out that Garret also played the harmonica, she knew their meeting was **kismet**.

synonym: destiny

· ·

to ridicule with satire

The mayor hated being **lampooned** by the press for his efforts to improve people's politeness.

synonyms: tease

BASIC

LAX
adj (laaks)

....

LECHEROUS
adj (<u>lehch</u> uh ruhs)

....

LILLIPUTIAN
noun (lihl ee <u>pyoo</u> shun)

not rigid, loose; negligent

Because our delivery boy is **lax,** the newspaper often arrives sopping wet.

synonyms: careless, imprecise

· ·

lewd, lustful

The school board censored the movie because of its portrayal of the **lecherous** criminal.

synonyms: lascivious, promiscuous

· ·

a very small person or thing

Next to her Amazonian roommate, the girl appeared to be **lilliputian.**

synonyms: diminutive, small

LIMBER
adj (<u>lihm</u> buhr)

....

LITHE
adj (lieth)

....

MALEVOLENT
adj (muh <u>lehv</u> uh luhnt)

flexible, capable of being shaped

After years of doing so much yoga, the elderly man was remarkably **limber**.

synonyms: agile, nimble

• •

moving and bending with ease; marked by effortless grace

The dancer's **lithe** movements proved her to be a rising star in the ballet corps.

synonyms: flexible, limber

• •

exhibiting ill will; wishing harm to others

The **malevolent** gossiper spread false rumors with frequency.

synonyms: malicious, hateful

BASIC

MALLEABLE
adj (<u>maal</u> ee uh buhl)

· ·

MASOCHIST
noun (<u>maas</u> uhk ihst)

· ·

MAVERICK
noun (<u>maav</u> rihk) (<u>maav</u> uh rihk)

BASIC

easily influenced or shaped, capable of being altered by outside forces

The welder heated the metal before shaping it because the heat made it **malleable**.

synonyms: adaptable, pliable

· ·

one who enjoys being subjected to pain or humiliation

Only a **masochist** would volunteer to take on this nightmarish project.

· ·

an independent individual who does not go along with a group

The senator was a **maverick** who was willing to vote against his own party's position.

synonym: nonconformist

BASIC

MEGALOMANIA
noun (<u>mehg</u> uh loh <u>may</u> nee uh)

· ·

MISSIVE
noun (<u>mihs</u> ihv)

· ·

MITIGATE
verb (<u>miht</u> ih gayt)

BASIC

obsession with great or grandiose performance

Many of the Roman emperors suffered from severe **megalomania**.

synonyms: egoism, self-centeredness

· ·

a written note or letter

Priscilla spent hours composing a romantic **missive** for Elvis.

synonym: message

· ·

to make less severe, make milder

A judge may **mitigate** a sentence if it's decided that the crime was committed out of necessity.

synonyms: relieve, alleviate

MODICUM
noun (<u>mahd</u> ih kuhm)

. . . .

MOROSE
adj (muh <u>rohs</u>) (maw <u>rohs</u>)

. . . .

MUTABILITY
noun (myoo tuh <u>bihl</u> uh tee)

BASIC

a small portion, limited quantity

I expect at least a **modicum** of assistance from you on the day of the party.

synonyms: crumb, iota

· ·

gloomy, sullen

After hearing that the internship had been given to someone else, Lenny was **morose** for days.

synonyms: pessimistic, dour

· ·

the quality of being capable of change, in form or character; susceptibility of change

The actress lacked the **mutability** needed to perform in the improvisational play.

synonyms: inconstancy, variation

MYOPIC
adj (mie <u>ahp</u> ihk) (mie <u>oh</u> pihk)

....

NEBULOUS
adj (<u>neh</u> <u>byoo</u> luhs)

....

NEFARIOUS
adj (nih <u>fahr</u> ee uhs)

lacking foresight, having a narrow view or long-range perspective

Not wanting to spend a lot of money up front, the **myopic** business owner would likely suffer the consequences later.

synonyms: short-sighted, unthinking

· ·

vague, undefined

The candidate's **nebulous** plans to fight crime made many voters skeptical.

synonyms: hazy, unclear

· ·

intensely wicked or vicous

Nefarious deeds are never far from an evil-doer's mind.

synonyms: malevolent, sinister

BASIC

NON SEQUITUR
noun (nahn <u>sehk</u> wih tuhr)

· ·

NOVEL
adj (<u>nah</u> vuhl)

· ·

OBSTINATE
adj (<u>ahb</u> stih nuht)

BASIC

a statement that does not follow logically from anything previously said

After the heated political debate, her comment about cake was a real **non sequitur**.

synonyms: illogical argument, off-topic comment

....

new and not resembling anything formerly known

Piercing any part of the body other than the earlobes was **novel** in the 1950s, but now it is quite common.

synonyms: original, innovative

....

unreasonably persistent

The **obstinate** journalist would not reveal his source, and thus, was jailed for 30 days.

synonyms: stubborn, headstrong

BASIC

OLFACTORY
adj (ohl <u>faak</u> tuh ree)

··

OPPORTUNIST
noun (aap ore <u>too</u> nist)

··

ORNERY
adj (<u>ohr</u> nuh ree)

relating to the sense of smell

Whenever she entered a candle store, her **olfactory** sense was awakened.

synonyms: fragrant, odorous

· ·

one who takes advantage of any opportunity to achieve an end, with little regard for principles

The **opportunist** wasted no time in stealing the idea and presenting it as his own.

synonyms: user, self-seeker

· ·

having an irritable disposition, cantankerous

My first impression of the taxi driver was that he was **ornery,** but then he explained that he'd just had a bad day.

synonyms: disagreeable, unfriendly

OSTRACIZE
verb (<u>ahs</u> truh size)

··

OUST
verb (owst)

··

PALTRY
adj (<u>pawl</u> tree)

to exclude from a group by common consent

Feeling **ostracized** from her friends, Tabitha couldn't figure out what she had done.

synonyms: isolate, excommunicate

· ·

to remove from position by force; eject

After President Nixon so offensively lied to the country during Watergate, he was **ousted** from office.

synonyms: dismiss, evict

· ·

pitifully small or worthless

Bernardo paid the ragged boy the **paltry** sum of 25 cents to carry his luggage all the way to the hotel.

synonyms: trifling, petty

BASIC

PARAGON
noun (<u>paar</u> uh gon)

· ·

PARAMOUNT
adj (<u>paar</u> uh mownt)

· ·

PARE
verb (payr)

a model of excellence or perfection

She's the **paragon** of what a judge should be: honest, intelligent, and just.

synonyms: ideal, paradigm

• •

supreme, of chief importance

It's of **paramount** importance that we make it back to camp before the storm hits.

synonyms: primary, dominant

• •

to trim off excess, reduce

The cook's hands were sore after she **pared** hundreds of potatoes for the banquet.

synonyms: peel, clip

BASIC

PARIAH
noun (puh <u>rie</u> ah)

∙∙∙

PATRONIZE
verb (<u>pay</u> troh niez)

∙∙∙

PENCHANT
noun (<u>pehn</u> chehnt)

an outcast

Once he betrayed those in his community, he was banished and lived the life of a **pariah**.

· ·

to act as patron of, to adopt an air of condescension toward; to buy from

LuAnn **patronized** the students, treating them like simpletons, which they deeply resented.

synonyms: condescend

· ·

an inclination, a definite liking

After Daniel visited the Grand Canyon, he developed a **penchant** for travel.

synonyms: leaning, predilection

PLAINTIVE
adj (<u>playn</u> tihv)

. . . .

PLUCKY
adj (<u>pluh</u> kee)

. . . .

PORE
verb (pohr)

expressive of suffering or woe, melancholy

The **plaintive** cries from the girl trapped in the tree were heard by all.

synonyms: mournful, sorrowful

• •

courageous; spunky

The **plucky** young nurse dove into the foxhole, determined to help the wounded soldier.

synonym: brave

• •

to read studiously or attentively

I've **pored** over this text, yet I still can't understand it.

synonym: fix attention on

PRECARIOUS
adj (prih <u>caa</u> ree uhs)

· ·

PRIMEVAL
adj (priem <u>ee</u> vuhl)

· ·

PROLIFERATE
verb (proh <u>lih</u> fuhr ayt)

BASIC

lacking in security or stability; dependent on chance or uncertain conditions

Given the **precarious** circumstances, I chose to opt out of the deal completely.

synonyms: doubtful, chancy

· ·

ancient, primitive

The archaeologist claimed that the skeleton was of **primeval** origin, though in fact it was the remains of a modern-day monkey.

synonyms: primordial, original

· ·

to grow by rapid production of new parts; increase in number

The cancer cells **proliferated** so quickly that even the doctor was surprised.

synonym: multiply

BASIC

PROPENSITY
noun (proh <u>pehn</u> suh tee)

....

PROXY
noun (<u>prahk</u> see)

....

PSEUDONYM
noun (<u>soo</u> duh nihm)

A natural inclination or preference

She has a **propensity** for lashing out at others when stressed, so we leave her alone when she's had a rough day.

synonym: tendency

••

a person authorized to act for someone else

In the event the stock shareholder can't attend the meeting, he'll send a **proxy**.

synonyms: representative, alternate

••

a fictitious name, used particularly by writers to conceal identity

Though George Eliot sounds as though it's a male name, it was the **pseudonym** that Marian Evans used when she published her classic novel *Middlemarch*.

synonym: pen name

PURLOIN
verb (<u>puhr</u> loyn)

....

RANKLE
verb (<u>raang</u> kuhl)

....

RAPT
adj (raapt)

to steal

The amateur detective Dupin found the **purloined** letter for which the police had searched in vain.

synonyms: pilfer, embezzle

· ·

to cause anger and irritation

At first the kid's singing was adorable, but after 40 minutes it began to **rankle**.

synonyms: embitter, annoy

· ·

deeply absorbed

The story was so well performed that the usually rowdy children were **rapt** until the final word.

synonyms: engrossed, immersed

BASIC

RAREFY
verb (<u>rayr</u> uh fie)

· ·

RAZE
verb (rayz)

· ·

REFUTE
verb (rih <u>fyoot</u>)

BASIC

to make rare, thin, or less dense

The atmosphere **rarefies** as altitude increases, so the air atop a mountain is too thin to breathe.

synonyms: attenuate, prune

· ·

to tear down, demolish

The house had been **razed**; where it once stood, there was nothing but splinters and bricks.

synonyms: level, destroy

· ·

to contradict, discredit

She made such a persuasive argument that nobody could **refute** it.

synonym: deny

REMISSION
noun (rih <u>mih</u> shuhn)

. . . .

REPLETE
adj (rih <u>pleet</u>)

. . . .

REPOSE
noun (rih <u>pohz</u>)

a lessening of intensity or degree

The doctor told me that the disease had gone into **remission**.

synonyms: abatement, subsiding

· ·

abundantly supplied, complete

The gigantic supermarket was **replete** with consumer products of every kind.

synonyms: abounding, full

· ·

relaxation, leisure

After working hard every day in the busy city, Mike finds his **repose** on weekends playing golf with friends.

synonyms: calmness, tranquility

REPREHENSIBLE
adj (rehp ree <u>hehn</u> suh buhl)

....

RESCIND
verb (rih <u>sihnd</u>)

....

RESILIENT
adj (rih <u>sihl</u> yuhnt)

blameworthy, disreputable

Lowell was thrown out of the bar because of his **reprehensible** behavior toward the other patrons.

synonyms: culpable, deplorable

· ·

to repeal, cancel

After the celebrity was involved in a scandal, the car company **rescinded** its offer of an endorsement contract.

synonyms: void, annul, revoke

· ·

able to recover quickly after illness or bad luck; able to bounce back to shape

Psychologists say that being **resilient** in life is one of the keys to success and happiness.

synonyms: flexible, elastic

BASIC

RESOLUTE
adj (<u>reh</u> suh <u>loot</u>)

· ·

RESPLENDENT
adj (rih <u>splehn</u> dihnt)

· ·

REVILE
verb (rih <u>veye</u> uhl)

marked by firm determination

Louise was **resolute**: She would get into medical school no matter what.

synonyms: firm, unwavering, intent

· ·

splendid, brilliant

The bride looked **resplendent** in her gown and sparkling tiara.

synonyms: dazzling, bright

· ·

to criticize with harsh language, verbally abuse

The artist's new installation was **reviled** by critics who weren't used to the departure from his usual work.

synonyms: vituperate, scold, assail

RHETORIC
noun (<u>reh</u> tuhr ihk)

· ·

RIFE
adj (rief)

· ·

SACCHARINE
adj (<u>saa</u> kuh ruhn)

the art of speaking or writing effectively; skill in the effective use of speech

Lincoln's talent for **rhetoric** was evident in his beautifully expressed Gettysburg Address.

synonyms: eloquence, articulateness

. . . .

abundant, prevalent, especially to an increasing degree; filled with

The essay was so **rife** with grammatical errors that it had to be rewritten.

synonyms: numerous, prevailing

. . . .

excessively sweet or sentimental

Geoffrey's **saccharine** poems nauseated Lucy, and she wished he'd stop sending them.

synonyms: maudlin, fulsome

SACRILEGIOUS
adj (<u>saak</u> rih <u>lihj</u> uhs)

....

SAVANT
noun (suh <u>vahnt</u>)

....

SECULAR
adj (<u>seh</u> kyoo luhr)

impious, irreverent toward what is held to be sacred or holy

It's considered **sacrilegious** for one to enter a mosque wearing shoes.

synonyms: profane, blasphemous

....

a person of learning; especially one with knowledge in a special field

The **savant** so impressed us with his knowledge that we asked him to come speak at our school.

synonym: scholar

....

not specifically pertaining to religion, relating to the world

Although his favorite book was the Bible, the archbishop also read **secular** works such as mysteries.

synonyms: temporal, material

SEQUESTER
verb (suh <u>kweh</u> stuhr)

· ·

SPARTAN
adj (<u>spahr</u> tihn)

· ·

SQUALID
adj (<u>skwa</u> lihd)

BASIC

to set apart, seclude

When juries are **sequestered**, it can take days, even weeks, to come up with a verdict.

synonyms: segregate, isolate

. . . .

highly self-disciplined; frugal, austere

When he was in training, the athlete preferred to live in a **spartan** room, so he could shut out all distractions.

synonyms: restrained, simple

. . . .

filthy and degraded as the result of neglect or poverty

The **squalid** living conditions in the building outraged the new tenants.

synonyms: unclean, foul

STYMIE
verb (<u>stie</u> mee)

....

SUBTERRANEAN
adj (<u>suhb</u> tuh <u>ray</u> nee uhn)

....

SULLY
verb (<u>suh</u> lee)

to block or thwart

The police effort to capture the bank robber was **stymied** when he escaped through a rear window.

synonyms: stump, baffle, foil

· ·

hidden, secret; underground

Subterranean tracks were created for the trains after it was decided they had run out of room above ground.

synonyms: buried, concealed, sunken

· ·

to tarnish, taint

With the help of a public-relations firm, he was able to restore his **sullied** reputation.

synonyms: defile, besmirch

SURMOUNT
verb (suhr <u>mownt</u>)

....

TACTILE
adj (<u>taak</u> tihl)

....

TAWDRY
adj (<u>taw</u> dree)

to conquer, overcome

The blind woman **surmounted** great obstacles to become a well-known trial lawyer.

synonyms: clear, hurdle, leap

· ·

producing a sensation of touch

The Museum of Natural History displays objects for people to touch so that they have a **tactile** understanding of how different peoples and animals lived.

synonyms: perceptible, tangible

· ·

gaudy, cheap, showy

The performer changed into her **tawdry** costume and stepped onto the stage.

synonyms: flashy, chintzy

TERSE
adj (tuhrs)

....

THWART
verb (thwahrt)

....

TOUT
verb (towt)

concise, brief, free of extra words

Her **terse** style of writing was widely praised by the editors, who had been used to seeing long-winded material.

synonyms: succinct, brusque

· ·

to block or prevent from happening; frustrate, defeat the hopes or aspirations of

Thwarted in its attempt to get at the bananas inside the box, the chimp began to squeal.

synonyms: oppose, foil, frustrate

· ·

to praise or publicize loudly or extravagantly

She **touted** her skills as superior to ours, though in fact, we were all at the same level.

synonyms: acclaim, proclaim

BASIC

TRAJECTORY
noun (truh <u>jehk</u> tuh ree)

· ·

TRANSIENT
adj (<u>traan</u> see uhnt)

· ·

TRANSITORY
adj (<u>traan</u> sih <u>tohr</u> ee)

BASIC

the path followed by a moving object, whether through space or otherwise; flight

The **trajectory** of the pitched ball was interrupted by an unexpected bird.

synonyms: path, route, course

· ·

passing with time, temporary, short-lived

The reporter lived a **transient** life, staying in one place only long enough to cover the current story.

synonyms: brief, transitory

· ·

short-lived, existing only briefly

The actress's popularity proved **transitory** when her play folded within the month.

synonyms: transient, ephemeral, momentary

UNCANNY
adj (uhn <u>kaa</u> nee)

. . . .

UNCONSCIONABLE
adj (uhn <u>kahn</u> shuhn uh buhl)

. . . .

VEHEMENTLY
adverb (<u>vee</u> ih mehnt lee)

BASIC

so keen and perceptive as to seem supernatural, peculiarly unsettling

Though they weren't related, their resemblance was **uncanny**.

synonyms: weird, eerie

. . . .

unscrupulous; shockingly unfair or unjust

After she promised me the project, the fact that she gave it to someone else is **unconscionable**.

synonyms: dishonorable, indefensible

. . . .

marked by extreme intensity of emotions or convictions

She **vehemently** opposed the closing of the neighborhood garden, and was even arrested for protesting when the bulldozers came.

synonyms: vociferously, unequivocally

BASIC

VERNACULAR
noun (vuhr <u>naa</u> kyoo luhr)

· ·

VICARIOUSLY
adverb (vie <u>kaar</u> ee uhs lee)

· ·

VINDICATE
verb (<u>vihn</u> dih kayt)

everyday language used by ordinary people; specialized language of a profession

Preeti could not understand the **vernacular** of the south, where she had recently moved.

synonyms: dialect, patois, lingo

• •

felt or undergone as if one were taking part in the experience or feelings of another

She lived **vicariously** through the characters in the adventure books she was always reading.

synonyms: substitute, delegated

• •

to clear of blame; support a claim

Tess felt **vindicated** when her prediction about the impending tornado came true.

synonyms: justify, exonerate

WANTON
adj (<u>wahn</u> tuhn)

. . . .

WIELD
verb (weeld)

. . . .

WILY
adj (<u>wie</u> lee)

BASIC

undisciplined, unrestrained, reckless

The order of the school was a much needed change from her former, **wanton** ways.

synonyms: capricious, lewd, licentious

• •

to exercise authority or influence effectively

For such a young congressman, he **wielded** a lot of power.

synonym: exert

• •

clever; deceptive

Yet again, the **wily** coyote managed to elude the ranchers who wanted it dead.

synonyms: cunning, tricky, crafty

WRY
adj (rie)

· ·

YEN
noun (yehn)

· ·

bent or twisted in shape or condition; dryly humorous

Every time she teased him, she shot her friends a **wry** smile.

synonyms: askew, sardonic

• •

a strong desire, craving

Pregnant women commonly have a **yen** for pickles.

synonym: desire

• •

ABET
verb (uh <u>beht</u>)

· ·

ABROGATE
verb (<u>aab</u> ruh gayt)

· ·

ACCEDE
verb (aak <u>seed</u>)

to aid; to act as an accomplice

While Derwin robbed the bank, Marvin **abetted** his friend by pulling up the getaway car.

synonyms: help, succor, assist

· ·

to annul; to abolish by authoritative action

The president's job is to **abrogate** any law that fosters inequality among citizens.

synonyms: nullify, revoke, repeal

· ·

to express approval, to agree to

Once the mayor heard the reasonable request, she happily **acceded** to the proposal.

synonyms: consent, concur

INTERMEDIATE

ACCLIVITY
noun (uh <u>klihv</u> ih tee)

· ·

ADJUDICATE
verb (uh <u>jood</u> ih kayt)

· ·

AERIE
noun (<u>ayr</u> ee) (<u>eer</u> ee)

an incline or upward slope, the ascending side of a hill

We were so tired from hiking that by the time we reached the **acclivity,** it looked more like a mountain than a hill.

synonyms: ascent, upgrade

· ·

to hear and settle a matter; to act as a judge

The principal **adjudicated** the disagreement between two students.

synonyms: arbitrate, mediate

· ·

a nest built high in the air; an elevated, often secluded, dwelling

Perched high among the trees, the eagle's **aerie** was filled with eggs.

synonyms: perch, stronghold

AFFECTED
adj (uh <u>fehk</u> tihd)

. . . .

AGGREGATE
noun (<u>aa</u> grih giht)

. . . .

ALIMENTARY
adj (aal uh <u>mehn</u> tuh ree)
(aal uh <u>mehn</u> tree)

INTERMEDIATE

phony, artificial

The **affected** hairdresser spouted French phrases, though she had never been to France.

synonyms: put-on, insincere, pretentious

· ·

a collective mass, the sum total

An **aggregate** of panic-stricken customers mobbed the bank, demanding their life savings.

synonyms: whole, entirety

· ·

pertaining to food, nutrition, or digestion

After a particularly good meal, Sherlock turned to his companion and exclaimed, "I feel quite good, very well fed. It was **alimentary** my dear Watson."

synonyms: nourishing, nutritive

INTERMEDIATE

AMORPHOUS
adj (ay mohr fuhs)

· ·

ANTHROPOMORPHIC
adj (aan thruh poh mohr fihk)

· ·

APOSTATE
noun (uh pahs tayt)

having no definite form

The Blob featured an **amorphous** creature that was constantly changing shape.

synonyms: shapeless, indistinct

· ·

suggesting human characteristics for animals and inanimate things

Many children's stories feature **anthropomorphic** animals such as talking wolves and pigs.

synonym: humanlike

· ·

one who renounces a religious faith

So that he could divorce his wife, he scoffed at the church doctrines and declared himself an **apostate**.

synonyms: traitor, defector, deserter

INTERMEDIATE

APPOSITE
adj (<u>aap</u> puh ziht)

....

ARCHIPELAGO
noun (ahr kuh <u>pehl</u> uh goh)

....

ARREARS
noun (uh <u>reerz</u>)

INTERMEDIATE

strikingly appropriate or well adapted

The lawyer presented an **apposite** argument upon cross-examining the star witness.

synonyms: apt, relevant, suitable

· ·

a large group of islands

Between villages in the Stockholm **archipelago**, boat taxis are the only form of transportation.

synonyms: cluster, scattering

· ·

unpaid, overdue debts or bills; neglected obligations

After the expensive lawsuit, Dominic's accounts were in **arrears**.

synonym: balance due

INTERMEDIATE

AUTOCRAT
noun (<u>aw</u> toh kraat)

....

AVER
verb (uh <u>vuhr</u>)

....

BALLAST
noun (<u>baal</u> uhst)

a dictator

Mussolini has been described as an **autocrat** who tolerated no opposition.

synonyms: tyrant, despot

••

to declare to be true, to affirm

"Yes, he was holding a gun," the witness **averred**.

synonyms: assert, attest

••

a structure that helps to stabilize or steady

Communication and honesty are the true **ballasts** of relationship.

synonyms: counterweight, balancer

BECALM
verb (bih <u>kahm</u>)

....

BECLOUD
verb (bih <u>klowd</u>)

....

BILIOUS
adj (<u>bihl</u> yuhs)

INTERMEDIATE

to stop the progress of, to soothe

The warm air **becalmed** the choppy waves.

synonyms: quiet, allay, still

. . . .

to make less visible, obscure, or blur

Her ambivalence about the long commute **beclouded** her enthusiasm about the job.

synonyms: muddle, cloud

. . . .

ill-tempered, sickly, ailing

The party ended early when the **bilious** 5-year-old tried to run off with the birthday's girl's presents.

synonyms: pale, feeble

INTERMEDIATE

BLITHELY
adv (<u>blieth</u> lee)

. . . .

BOMBASTIC
adj (bahm <u>baast</u> ihk)

. . . .

BURNISH
verb (<u>buhr</u> nihsh)

merrily, lightheartedly cheerful; without appropriate thought

Wanting to redecorate the office, she **blithely** assumed her co-workers wouldn't mind and moved the furniture in the space.

synonyms: in a carefree manner

. . . .

high-sounding but meaningless; ostentatiously lofty in style

Mussolini's speeches were mostly **bombastic**; his outrageous claims had no basis in fact.

synonyms: grandiose, inflated

. . . .

to polish; to make smooth and bright

Mr. Frumpkin loved to stand in the sun and **burnish** his luxury car.

synonyms: shine, buff

INTERMEDIATE

BURSAR
noun (<u>buhr</u> suhr) (<u>buhr</u> sahr)

· ·

CAUSTIC
adj (<u>kah</u> stihk)

· ·

CEDE
verb (seed)

INTERMEDIATE

a keeper of funds

The **bursar** of the school was in charge of allocating all scholarship funds.

synonym: treasurer

. . . .

biting, sarcastic

Writer Dorothy Parker gained her reputation for **caustic** wit, and her tombstone is inscribed with a fittingly clever "Excuse my dust."

synonyms: sardonic, incisive

. . . .

to surrender possession of something

Argentina **ceded** the Falkland Islands to Britain after a brief war.

synonyms: resign, yield, relinquish

INTERMEDIATE

CERTITUDE
noun (<u>suhr</u> tih tood)

....

CIRCUITOUS
adj (suhr <u>kyoo</u> ih tuhs)

....

CLOYING
adj (<u>kloy</u> ing)

assurance, freedom from doubt

The witness' **certitude** about the night in question had a big impact on the jury.

synonyms: certainty, conviction

• •

indirect, roundabout

The venue was only a short walk from the train station, but a roadblock meant I had to take a **circuitous** route.

synonyms: lengthy, devious

• •

sickly sweet; excessive

When Dave and Liz got together, their **cloying** affection towards one another often made their friends ill.

synonyms: excessive, fulsome

INTERMEDIATE

CONCORD
noun (<u>kahn</u> kohrd)

....

CONTENTIOUS
adj (kuhn <u>tehn</u> shuhs)

....

CONVERGENCE
noun (kuhn <u>vehr</u> juhns)

INTERMEDIATE

agreement

The sisters are now in **concord** about the car they had to share.

synonyms: accord, concurrence

• •

quarrelsome, disagreeable, belligerent

The **contentious** gentleman in the bar ridiculed anything anyone said.

synonyms: argumentative, fractious, litigious

• •

the state of separate elements joining or coming together

A **convergence** of factors led to the tragic unfolding of World War I.

synonyms: union, concurrence, coincidence

INTERMEDIATE

COQUETTE
noun (koh <u>keht</u>)

. . . .

CULL
verb (kuhl)

. . . .

DEARTH
noun (duhrth)

INTERMEDIATE

a flirtatious woman

The librarian could turn into a **coquette** just by letting her hair down and changing the swing of her hips.

synonym: flirt

• •

to select, weed out

You should **cull** the words you need to study from all the flash cards.

synonyms: pick, extract

• •

lack, scarcity, insufficiency

The **dearth** of supplies in our city made it difficult to survive the blizzard.

synonyms: absence, shortage

INTERMEDIATE

DENIZEN
noun (<u>dehn</u> ih zihn)

. . . .

DERIDE
verb (dih <u>ried</u>)

. . . .

DILAPIDATED
adj (dih <u>laap</u> ih dayt ihd)

a resident

The **denizens** of the state understandably wanted to select their own leaders.

synonym: inhabitant

· ·

to laugh at contemptuously, to make fun of

As soon as Jorge heard the others **deriding** Anthony, he came to his defense.

synonyms: ridicule

· ·

in disrepair, run down

Rather than get discouraged, the architect saw great potential in the **dilapidated** house.

synonyms: decayed, fallen into partial ruin

DISINGENUOUS
adj (<u>dihs</u> ihn <u>jehn</u> yoo uhs)

···

DISINTERESTED
adj (dihs <u>ihn</u> trih stihd)
(dihs <u>ihn</u> tuh reh stihd)

···

DISPASSIONATE
adj (dihs <u>paash</u> ih niht)

giving a false appearance of simple frankness; misleading

It was **disingenuous** of him to suggest that he had no idea of the requests made by his campaign contributors.

synonyms: insincere, tricky

••

fair-minded, unbiased

A fair trial is made possible by the selection of **disinterested** jurors.

synonyms: impartial, unprejudiced

••

unaffected by bias or strong emotions; not personally or emotionally involved in something

Ideally, photographers should be **dispassionate** observers of what goes on in the world.

synonyms: disinterested, impartial

DOGGED
adj (<u>daw</u> guhd)

. . . .

DOLEFUL
adj (<u>dohl</u> fuhl)

. . . .

DOUR
adj (<u>doo</u> uhr) (<u>dow</u> uhr)

INTERMEDIATE

✓

stubbornly persevering

The police inspector's **dogged** determination helped him catch the thief.

synonyms: tenacious, obstinate

••

sad, mournful

Looking into the **doleful** eyes of the lonely pony, the girl yearned to take him home.

synonyms: dejected, woeful

••

sullen and gloomy; stern and severe

The **dour** hotel concierge demanded payment for the room in advance.

synonyms: austere, strict, grave

INTERMEDIATE

EMOLLIENT
adj (ih <u>mohl</u> yuhnt)

....

EMULATE
verb (<u>ehm</u> yuh layt)

....

ENCUMBER
verb (ehn <u>kuhm</u> buhr)

INTERMEDIATE

soothing, especially to the skin

After being out in the sun for so long, the **emollient** cream was a welcome relief on my skin.

synonyms: softening, mollifying

• •

to strive to equal or excel, to imitate

Children often **emulate** their parents.

synonyms: follow, mimic

• •

to weigh down, to burden

She brought only her laptop to the cabin, where she wrote **unencumbered** by the distractions of the city.

synonym: to hamper the activity of

ENJOIN
verb (ehn <u>joyn</u>)

....

ESCHEW
verb (ehs <u>choo</u>)

....

ESPOUSE
verb (ih <u>spowz</u>)

INTERMEDIATE

to direct or impose with urgent appeal, to order with emphasis; to forbid

Patel is **enjoined** by his culture from eating the flesh of a cow, which is sacred in India.

synonyms: instruct, charge

. . . .

to shun; to avoid (as something wrong or distasteful)

The filmmaker **eschewed** artifical light for her actors, resulting in a stark movie style.

synonyms: evade, escape

. . . .

to take up and support as a cause; to marry

Because of his religious beliefs, the preacher could not **espouse** the use of capital punishment.

synonyms: champion, adopt

ESPY
verb (ehs <u>peye</u>)

....

EUPHEMISM
noun (<u>yoo</u> fuh mihz uhm)

....

EXPONENT
noun (<u>ehk</u> spoh nuhnt)

to catch sight of, glimpse

Amidst a crowd in black clothing, she **espied** the colorful dress that her friend was wearing.

synonym: discern

• •

an inoffensive and agreeable expression that is substituted for one that is considered offensive

The funeral director preferred to use the **euphemism** "passed away" instead of the word "dead."

• •

one who champions or advocates

The vice president was an enthusiastic **exponent** of computer technology.

synonyms: supporter, representative

INTERMEDIATE

EXPOUND
verb (ihk <u>spownd</u>)

....

FACETIOUS
adj (fuh <u>see</u> shuhs)

....

FACILE
adj (<u>faa</u> suhl)

to explain or describe in detail

The teacher **expounded** on the theory of relativity for hours.

synonyms: elucidate, elaborate

· ·

witty, humorous

Her **facetious** remarks made the uninteresting meeting more lively.

synonyms: amusing, comical

· ·

easily accomplished; seeming to lack sincerity or depth; arrived at without due effort

Given the complexity of the problem, it seemed a rather **facile** solution.

synonyms: effortless, superficial

INTERMEDIATE

FLIPPANT
adj (<u>flihp</u> uhnt)

∙∙

FLOUT
verb (flowt)

∙∙

FODDER
noun (<u>fohd</u> uhr)

marked by disrespectful lightheartedness or casualness

Her **flippant** response was unacceptable and she was asked again to explain herself.

synonyms: pert, disrespectful

• •

to scorn, to disregard with contempt

The protestors **flouted** the committee's decision and hoped to sway public opinion.

synonyms: mock, sneer, spurn

• •

raw material, as for artistic creation, readily abundant ideas or images

The governor's hilarious blunder was good **fodder** for the comedian.

FOREGO
verb (fohr <u>goh</u>)

. . . .

FORTITUDE
noun (<u>fohr</u> tih tood)

. . . .

FURLOUGH
noun (<u>fuhr</u> loh)

INTERMEDIATE

to go before

Because of the risks of the expedition, the team leader made sure to **forego** the climbers.

synonym: precede

....

strength of mind that allows one to encounter adversity with courage

Months in the trenches exacted great **fortitude** of the soldiers.

synonyms: endurance, courage

....

a leave of absence, especially granted to soldier or a prisoner

After seeing months of combat, the soldier received a much-deserved **furlough**.

synonym: time off

INTERMEDIATE

FURTIVE
adj (<u>fuhr</u> tihv)

....

GROTTO
noun (<u>grah</u> toh)

....

HEDONIST
noun (<u>hee</u> duhn ihst)

INTERMEDIATE

sly, with hidden motives

The **furtive** glances they exchanged made me suspect they were up to something.

synonyms: secret, surreptitious

· ·

a small cave

Alone on the island, Philoctetes sought shelter in a **grotto**.

synonyms: cavern, recess, burrow

· ·

one who pursues pleasure as a goal

Michelle, an admitted **hedonist**, lays on the couch eating cookies every Saturday.

synonyms: pleasure-seeker, glutton

INTERMEDIATE

IMBIBE
verb (ihm bieb)

....

IMPASSIVE
adj (ihm pahs sihv)

....

IMPUDENT
adj (ihm pyuh duhnt)

INTERMEDIATE

to receive into the mind and take in, absorb

If I always attend class, I can **imbibe** as much knowledge as possible.

synonym: absorb

· ·

absent of any external sign of emotion, expressionless

Given his **impassive** expression, it was hard to tell whether he approved of my plan.

synonyms: apathetic, unemotional

· ·

marked by cocky boldness or disregard for others

Considering the judge had been lenient in her sentence, it was **impudent** of the defendant to refer to her by her first name.

synonyms: arrogant, insolent

INTERMEDIATE

IMPUGN
verb (ihm <u>pyoon</u>)

· ·

INCIPIENT
adj (ihn <u>sihp</u> ee uhnt)

· ·

INHERENT
adj (ihn <u>hehr</u> ehnt)

INTERMEDIATE

to call into question; to attack verbally

"How dare you **impugn** my motives?" protested the lawyer, on being accused of ambulance chasing.

synonyms: challenge, dispute

• •

beginning to exist or appear; in an initial stage

The **incipient** idea seemed brilliant, but they knew it needed much more development.

synonyms: developing, basic

• •

involved essential character of something, built-in, inborn

The class was dazzled by the experiment and as a result more likely to remember the **inherent** scientific principle.

synonym: intrinsic

INQUEST
noun (<u>ihn</u> kwehst)

· ·

INSULAR
adj (<u>ihn</u> suh luhr) (<u>ihn</u> syuh luhr)

· ·

INTER
verb (ihn <u>tuhr</u>)

INTERMEDIATE

an investigation

The police chief ordered an **inquest** to determine what went wrong.

synonym: inquiry

• •

characteristic of an isolated people, especially having a narrow viewpoint

It was a shock for Kendra to go from her small high school, with her **insular** group of friends, to a huge college with students from all over the country.

synonyms: provincial, narrow-minded

• •

to bury

After giving the masses one last chance to pay their respects, the leader's body was **interred**.

INTERMEDIATE

INTRACTABLE
adj (ihn <u>traak</u> tuh buhl)

....

INTRANSIGENT
adj (ihn <u>traan</u> suh juhnt)
(ihn <u>traan</u> zuh juhnt)

....

INTREPID
adj (ihn <u>trehp</u> ihd)

INTERMEDIATE

not easily managed or manipulated

Intractable for hours, the wild horse eventually allowed the rider to mount.

synonyms: stubborn, unruly

. . . .

uncompromising, refusing to abandon an extreme position

His **intransigent** positions on social issues cost him the election.

synonyms: obstinate, unyielding

. . . .

fearless, resolutely courageous

Despite freezing winds, the **intrepid** hiker completed his ascent.

synonym: brave

INTERMEDIATE

INUNDATE
verb (<u>ihn</u> uhn dayt)

···

ITINERANT
adj (ie <u>tihn</u> uhr uhnt)

···

LAUDABLE
adj (<u>law</u> duh buhl)

to cover with a flood; to overwhelm as if with
a flood

The box office was **inundated** with requests for
tickets to the award-winning play.

synonyms: swamp, drown

• •

wandering from place to place; unsettled

The **itinerant** tomcat came back to the Johansson
homestead every two months.

synonyms: nomadic, vagrant

• •

deserving of praise

Kristin's dedication is **laudable,** but she doesn't
have the necessary skills to be a good paralegal.

synonyms: commendable, admirable

INTERMEDIATE

LEVITY
noun (<u>leh</u> vih tee)

. . . .

LIBERTARIAN
noun (lih buhr <u>tehr</u> ee uhn)

. . . .

LIBERTINE
noun (<u>lihb</u> uhr teen)

an inappropriate lack of seriousness, overly casual

The joke added needed **levity** to the otherwise serious meeting.

synonyms: amusement, humor

• •

one who advocates individual rights and free will

The **libertarian** was always at odds with the conservatives.

• •

a free thinker, usually used disparagingly; one without moral restraint

The **libertine** took pleasure in gambling away his family's money.

synonym: hedonist

INTERMEDIATE

MALAISE
noun (maa <u>layz</u>)

. . . .

MALEDICTION
noun (maal ih <u>dihk</u> shun)

. . . .

MANNERED
adj (<u>maan</u> uhrd)

a feeling of unease or depression

During his presidency, Jimmy Carter spoke of a "national **malaise**" and was subsequently criticized for being too negative.

synonyms: discomfort, unhappiness

· ·

a wish of evil upon another

The frog prince looked for a princess to kiss him and put an end to the witch's **malediction**.

synonym: curse

· ·

artificial or stilted in character

The portrait is an example of the **mannered** style that was favored in that era.

synonyms: affected, unnatural

INTERMEDIATE

MICROCOSM
noun (mie kruh kahz uhm)

· ·

MISANTHROPE
noun (mihs ahn throhp)

· ·

MISNOMER
noun (mihs noh muhr)

INTERMEDIATE

a small scale representation of a larger system

This department is in fact a **microcosm** of the entire corporation.

· ·

a person who hates or distrusts mankind

Scrooge was such a **misanthrope** that even the sight of children singing made him angry.

synonym: curmudgeon

· ·

an error in naming a person or place

Iceland is a **misnomer** since it isn't really icy; the name means "island."

synonyms: error, misapplication

MOLLIFY
verb (<u>mahl</u> uh fie)

· ·

NECROMANCY
noun (<u>nehk</u> ruh maan see)

· ·

NIHILISM
noun (<u>nie</u> hihl iz uhm)

to soothe in temper or disposition

A small raise and increased break time **mollified** the unhappy staff, at least for the moment.

synonyms: pacify, appease

• •

the practice of communicating with the dead in order to predict the future

The practice of **necromancy** supposes belief in survival of the soul after death.

synonyms: sorcery, black magic

• •

belief that traditional values and beliefs are unfounded and that existence is useless; belief that conditions in the social organization are so bad as to make destruction desirable

Robert's **nihilism** expressed itself in his lack of concern with the norms of moral society.

synonyms: skepticism, terrorism

OLIGARCHY
noun (<u>oh</u> lih gaar kee)

....

ONUS
noun (<u>oh</u> nuhs)

....

OPINE
verb (oh <u>pien</u>)

a government in which a small group exercises supreme control

In an **oligarchy,** the few who rule are generally wealthier and have more status than the others.

synonym: small government

• •

a burden, an obligation

Antonia was beginning to feel the **onus** of having to feed her friend's cat for the month.

synonyms: responsibility, hardship

• •

to express an opinion

At the "Let's Chat Talk Show," the audience member **opined** that the guest was in the wrong.

synonym: point out

INTERMEDIATE

OSCILLATE
verb (<u>ah</u> sihl ayt)

· ·

PAEAN
noun (<u>pee</u> uhn)

· ·

PALATIAL
adj (puh <u>lay</u> shuhl)

INTERMEDIATE

to swing back and forth like a pendulum; to vary between opposing beliefs or feelings

The move meant a new house in a lovely neighborhood, but she missed her friends, so she **oscillated** between joy and sadness.

synonyms: fluctuate, vary

. . . .

a song or expression of praise

He considered his newest painting a **paean** to his late wife.

synonym: tribute

. . . .

relating to a palace; magnificent

After living in a cramped studio apartment for years, Alicia thought the modest one bedroom looked downright **palatial**.

synonyms: grand, stately

INTERMEDIATE

PALPABLE
adj (<u>pahlp</u> uh buhl)

• •

PANACHE
noun (puh <u>nahsh</u>)

• •

PANDEMIC
adj (paan <u>deh</u> mihk)

INTERMEDIATE

capable of being touched or felt; easily perceived

The tension was **palpable** as I walked into the room.

synonyms: readily detected, tangible

· ·

flamboyance or dash in style and action

Leah has such **panache** when planning parties, even when they're last-minute affairs.

synonym: flair

· ·

occurring over a wide geographic area and affecting a large portion of the population

Pandemic alarm spread throughout Colombia after the devastating earthquake.

synonyms: general, extensive

PARADIGM
noun (<u>paar</u> uh diem)

· ·

PATENT
adj (<u>paa</u> tehnt)

· ·

PATHOGENIC
adj (paa thoh <u>jehn</u> ihk)

INTERMEDIATE

an outstandingly clear or typical example

The new restaurant owner used the fast-food giant as a **paradigm** for expansion into new locales.

synonym: model

• •

obvious, evident

Moe could no longer stand Frank's **patent** fawning over the boss and so confronted him.

synonyms: unconcealed, clear

• •

causing disease

Bina's research on the origins of **pathogenic** microorganisms should help stop the spread of disease.

synonyms: noxious, infecting

INTERMEDIATE

PATRICIAN
adj (puh <u>trih</u> shuhn)

···

PENITENT
adj (<u>peh</u> nih tehnt)

···

PHALANX
noun (<u>fay</u> laanks)

aristocratic

Though he really couldn't afford an expensive lifestyle, Claudius had **patrician** tastes.

synonym: high-class

· ·

expressing sorrow for sins or offenses, repentant

Claiming the murderer did not feel **penitent**, the victim's family felt his pardon should be denied.

synonyms: remorseful, apologetic

· ·

a compact or close-knit body of people, animals, or things

A **phalanx** of guards stood outside the prime minister's home day and night.

synonyms: mass, legion

INTERMEDIATE

PHILISTINE
noun (<u>fihl</u> uh steen)

··

PHLEGMATIC
adj (flehg <u>maa</u> tihk)

··

PIQUE
verb (peek)

INTERMEDIATE

a person who is guided by materialism and is disdainful of intellectual or artistic values

The **philistine** never even glanced at the rare violin in his collection but instead kept an eye on its value and sold it at a profit.

synonyms: lowbrow, materialist

....

having a sluggish, unemotional temperament

His writing was energetic but his **phlegmatic** personality wasn't suited for television, so he turned down the interview.

synonyms: matter-of-fact, undemonstrative

....

to arouse anger or resentment in; provoke

His continual insensitivity **piqued** my anger.

synonyms: irritate, rouse

INTERMEDIATE

PLATITUDE
noun (<u>plaa</u> tuh tood)

....

PLEBEIAN
adj (plee <u>bee</u> uhn)

....

POLITIC
adj (<u>pah</u> luh tihk)

overused and trite remark

Instead of the usual **platitudes,** the comedian gave a memorable and inspiring speech to the graduating class.

synonym: cliché

• •

crude or coarse; characteristic of commoners

After five weeks of rigorous studying, the graduate settled in for a weekend of **plebeian** socializing and television watching.

synonyms: unrefined, conventional

• •

shrewd and crafty in managing or dealing with things

She was wise to curb her tongue and was able to explain her problem to the judge in a respectful and **politic** manner.

synonym: tactful

PORTENTOUS
adj (pohr <u>tehn</u> tuhs)

• •

POSIT
verb (<u>pohz</u> iht)

• •

POTABLE
adj (<u>poh</u> tuh buhl)

foreshadowing, ominous; eliciting amazement and wonder

Everyone thought the rays of light were **portentous** until they realized a nine-year-old was playing a joke on them.

synonym: premonitory

•••

to assume as real or conceded; propose as an explanation

Before proving the math formula, we needed to **posit** that x and y were real numbers.

synonym: suggest

•••

suitable for drinking

Though the water was **potable**, it tasted terrible.

synonym: unpolluted

PRECIPITOUS
adj (pree <u>sih</u> puh tuhs)

∙∙

PRESAGE
noun (<u>preh</u> sihj)

∙∙

PRETERNATURAL
adj (pree tuhr <u>naach</u> uhr uhl)

steeply; hastily

At the sight of the approaching helicopters, Private Johnson **precipitously** shot a flare into the air.

synonyms: impetuous, headlong, reckless

• •

something that foreshadows; a feeling of what will happen in the future

The demolition of the Berlin Wall was a **presage** to the fall of the Soviet Union.

synonym: premonition

• •

existing outside of nature; extraordinary; supernatural

We were all amazed at her **preternatural** ability to recall smells from her early childhood.

synonyms: psychic, abnormal

INTERMEDIATE

PRODIGAL
adj (<u>prah</u> dih guhl)

· ·

PROFFER
verb (<u>prahf</u> uhr)

· ·

PROGENITOR
noun (proh <u>jehn</u> uh tuhr)

recklessly extravagant, wasteful

The **prodigal** expenditures on the military budget during a time of peace created a stir in the Cabinet.

synonym: lavish

· ·

to offer for acceptance

The deal **proffered** by the committee satisfied all those at the meeting, ending a month-long discussion.

synonym: propose

· ·

an ancestor in the direct line, forefather; founder

Though his parents had been born here, his **progenitors** were from India.

synonym: inventor

PROSAIC
adj (proh <u>say</u> ihk)

· ·

PROSTRATE
adj (<u>prah</u> strayt)

· ·

PROVINCIAL
adj (pruh <u>vihn</u> shuhl)

relating to prose (as opposed to poetry); dull, ordinary

Simon's **prosaic** style bored his writing teacher to tears, though he thought he had an artistic flair.

synonyms: unimaginative, everyday

• •

lying face downward in adoration or submission

Lying **prostrate** awaiting the Pope, a car splashed me with water.

synonym: submissive

• •

limited in outlook, narrow, unsophisticated

Having grown up in the city, Anita sneered at the **provincial** attitudes of her country cousins.

synonyms: unpolished, unrefined

INTERMEDIATE

PUGILISM
noun (<u>pyoo</u> juhl ih suhm)

....

PUNDIT
noun (<u>puhn</u> diht)

....

PURPORT
verb (puhr <u>pohrt</u>)

INTERMEDIATE

boxing

Pugilism has been defended as a positive outlet for aggressive impulses.

synonyms: sparring, fighting

....

one who gives opinions in an authoritative manner

The **pundits** on television are often more entertaining than the sitcoms.

synonym: critic

....

to profess, suppose, claim

Brad **purported** to be an opera lover, but he fell asleep at every performance he attended.

synonyms: pretend, purpose

RANCOR
noun (<u>raan</u> kuhr)

. . . .

REACTIONARY
adj (ree <u>aak</u> shuhn <u>ayr</u> ee)

. . . .

REFRACT
verb (rih <u>fraakt</u>)

bitter hatred

Having been teased mercilessly for years, Herb became filled with **rancor** toward those who had humiliated him.

synonym: deep-seated ill will

• •

marked by extreme conservatism, especially in politics

The former radical hippie had turned into quite a **reactionary,** and the press tried to expose her as a hypocrite.

synonyms: ultraconservative, right-wing, orthodox

• •

to deflect sound or light

The crystal **refracted** the rays of sunlight so they formed a beautiful pattern on the wall.

synonyms: bend, slant

INTERMEDIATE

RELEGATE
verb (<u>reh</u> luh <u>gayt</u>)

· ·

REMUNERATION
noun (rih <u>myoo</u> nuh ray shuhn)

· ·

REPROVE
verb (rih <u>proov</u>)

to send into exile, banish; assign

Because he hadn't scored any goals during the season, Abe was **relegated** to the bench for the championship game.

synonyms: consign, classify, refer

· ·

payment for goods or services or to recompense for losses

You can't expect people to do this kind of boring work without some form of **remuneration.**

synonyms: recompense, pay

· ·

to criticize or correct, usually in a gentle manner

Mrs. Hernandez **reproved** her daughter for staying out late and not calling.

synonyms: rebuke, admonish, reprimand

INTERMEDIATE

REQUITE
verb (rih <u>kwiet</u>)

....

SALACIOUS
adj (suh <u>lay</u> shuhs)

....

SALIENT
adj (<u>say</u> lee uhnt)

INTERMEDIATE

to return or repay

Thanks for offering to lend me $1,000, but I know I'll never be able to **requite** your generosity.

synonyms: reciprocate, compensate

· ·

appealing to sexual desire

His television character was wholesomely funny so audiences who saw his stand-up comedy routine were shocked by how **salacious** his jokes were.

synonym: lustful

· ·

prominent, of notable significance

His most **salient** characteristic is his tendency to dominate every conversation.

synonyms: noticeable, marked, outstanding

SATIATE
verb (<u>say</u> shee ayt)

....

SCRUPULOUS
adj (<u>skroop</u> yuh luhs)

....

SEAMY
adj (<u>see</u> mee)

INTERMEDIATE

to satisfy (as a need or desire) fully or to excess

After years of journeying around the world with nothing but backpacks, the friends had finally **satiated** their desire to travel.

synonym: gorge

· ·

acting in strict regard for what is considered proper; punctiliously exact

After the storm had destroyed their antique lamp, the Millers worked to repair it with **scrupulous** care.

synonyms: painstaking, meticulous

· ·

morally degraded, unpleasant

The tour guide avoided the **seamy** parts of town.

synonyms: sordid, sleazy

INTERMEDIATE

SIMIAN
adj (<u>sih</u> mee uhn)

....

SOJOURN
noun (<u>soh</u> juhrn)

....

SOPHOMORIC
adj (sahf <u>mohr</u> ihk)

apelike; relating to apes

Early man was more **simian** in appearance than is modern man.

synonyms: anthropoid, primate

•••

a temporary stay

After graduating from college, Iliani embarked on a **sojourn** to China.

synonym: visit

•••

exhibiting great immaturity and lack of judgment

After Sean's **sophomoric** behavior, he was grounded for weeks.

synonym: juvenile

INTERMEDIATE

SPORTIVE
adj (<u>spohr</u> tihv)

••

STALWART
adj (<u>stahl</u> wuhrt)

••

STINT
verb (stihnt)

frolicsome, playful

The lakeside vacation meant more **sportive** opportunities for the kids than the wine tour through France.

synonyms: frisky, merry

· ·

marked by outstanding strength and vigor of body, mind, or spirit

The 85-year old went to the market every day, impressing her neighbors with her **stalwart** routine.

synonyms: strong, bold

· ·

to be sparing or frugal; to restrict with respect to a share or allowance

Don't **stint** on the mayonnaise, because I don't like my sandwich too dry.

synonyms: skimp, scrimp

STIPULATE
verb (<u>stihp</u> yuh <u>layt</u>)

· ·

STRINGENT
adj (<u>strihn</u> guhnt)

· ·

SUPERSEDE
verb (<u>soo</u> puhr <u>seed</u>)

INTERMEDIATE

to specify as a condition or requirement of an agreement or offer

The contract **stipulated** that if the movie was never filmed, the actress got paid anyway.

synonyms: specifize, detail, designate

••

imposing severe, rigorous standards

Many people found it difficult to live up to the **stringent** moral standards imposed by the Puritans.

synonyms: restricted, tight, demanding

••

to cause to be set aside; to force out of use as inferior, replace

Her computer was still running version 2.0 of the software, which had long since been **superseded** by at least three more versions.

synonym: supplant

TEMPESTUOUS
adj (tehm <u>pehs</u> choo uhs)

. . . .

TENACIOUS
adj (teh <u>nay</u> shuhs)

. . . .

TENET
noun (<u>teh</u> niht)

INTERMEDIATE

stormy, turbulent

Our camping trip was cut short when the sun shower we were expecting turned into a **tempestuous** downpour.

synonyms: tumultuous, blustery

• •

tending to persist or cling; persistent in adhering to something valued or habitual

For years, against all odds, women **tenaciously** fought for the right to vote.

synonyms: stubborn, dogged, obstinate

• •

a principle, belief, or doctrine accepted by members of a group

One of the **tenets** of Islam is that it is not acceptable to eat pork.

synonym: canon

INTERMEDIATE

TREMULOUS
adj (<u>treh</u> myoo luhs)

. . . .

TROUNCE
verb (trowns)

. . . .

UNFROCK
verb (uhn <u>frahk</u>)

INTERMEDIATE

trembling, timid; easily shaken

The **tremulous** kitten had been separated from her mother.

synonyms: shaking, timorous, anxious

• •

to beat severely, defeat

The inexperienced young boxer was **trounced** in a matter of minutes.

synonyms: vanquish, conquer

• •

to dethrone, especially of priestly power

Any priest caught sullying the good name of his profession would certainly be **unfrocked**.

synonyms: demote, degrade

INTERMEDIATE

VERACITY
noun (vuhr <u>aa</u> sih tee)

• •

VERBOSE
adj (vuhr <u>bohs</u>)

• •

VERITABLE
adj (<u>vehr</u> iht uh buhl)

accuracy, truth

She had a reputation for **veracity,** so everyone believed her version of the story.

synonyms: truthfulness, reliability

· ·

wordy

The DNA analyst's answer was so **verbose** that the jury had trouble grasping his point.

synonyms: loquacious, garrulous

· ·

being without question, often used figuratively

The annual sale at the trendy boutique was a **veritable** madhouse of grasping shoppers.

synonyms: authentic, bona fide

INTERMEDIATE

VILIFY
verb (<u>vih</u> lih fie)

. . . .

VIRULENT
adj (<u>veer</u> yuh luhnt)

. . . .

VISCERAL
adj (<u>vihs</u> uhr uhl)

INTERMEDIATE

to slander, defame

As gossip columnists often **vilify** celebrities, they're usually held in low regard.

synonym: malign

• •

extremely poisonous; malignant; hateful

Alarmed at the **virulent** press he was receiving, the militant activist decided to go underground.

synonyms: infectious, toxic

• •

instinctive, not intellectual; deep, emotional

When my twin was wounded many miles away, I, too, had a **visceral** reaction.

synonyms: gut, earthy

INTERMEDIATE

VOLLEY
noun (<u>vah</u> lee)

....

WAN
adj (wahn)

....

WINSOME
adj (<u>wihn</u> suhm)

a flight of missiles; round of gunshots

The troops fired a **volley** of bullets at the enemy, but they couldn't be sure how many hit their target.

synonyms: discharge, barrage

• •

sickly pale

The sick child had a **wan** face, in contrast to her rosy-cheeked sister.

synonyms: ashen, sickly

• •

charming, happily engaging

Dawn gave the customs officers a **winsome** smile, and they let her pass without searching her bags.

synonyms: attractive, delightful

INTERMEDIATE

WORST
verb (wuhrst)

....

to gain the advantage over, defeat

The North **worsted** the South in America's Civil War.

synonyms: beat, vanquish

• •

INTERMEDIATE

ABATE
verb (uh <u>bayt</u>)

....

ABJURE
verb (aab <u>joor</u>)

....

ABNEGATE
verb (<u>aab</u> nih gayt)

to decrease, to reduce

My hunger **abated** when I saw how filthy the chef's hands were.

synonyms: dwindle, ebb, recede

• •

to renounce under oath, to abandon forever; to abstain from

After having been devout for most of his life, he suddenly **abjured** his beliefs, much to his family's disappointment.

synonyms: renounce, disavow

• •

to give up; to deny to oneself

After his retirement, the former police commissioner found it difficult to **abnegate** authority.

synonyms: abjure, surrender, renounce

ADVANCED

ABSTEMIOUS
adj (aab <u>stee</u> mee uhs)

· ·

ADJURE
verb (uh <u>joor</u>)

· ·

ADROIT
adj (uh <u>droyt</u>)

done sparingly; consuming in moderation

The spa served no sugar or wheat, but the clients found the retreat so calm that they didn't mind the **abstemious** rules.

synonyms: moderate, sparing, abstinent

• •

to appeal to

The criminal **adjured** to the court for mercy.

synonyms: beg, plead

• •

skillful; accomplished; highly competent

The **adroit** athlete completed even the most difficult obstacle course with ease.

synonyms: dexterous, proficient

ADUMBRATE
verb (<u>aad</u> uhm brayt) (uh <u>duhm</u> brayt)

···

ANIMUS
noun (<u>aan</u> uh muhs)

···

ANODYNE
noun (<u>aan</u> uh dyen)

to give a hint or indication of something to come

Her constant complaining about the job **adumbrated** her intent to leave.

synonyms: foreshadow, suggest

• •

a feeling of animosity or ill will

Though her teacher had failed her, she displayed no **animus** toward him.

synonyms: hostility, animosity

• •

a source of comfort; a medicine that relieves pain

The sound of classical music is usually just the **anodyne** I need after a tough day at work.

synonyms: analgesic, painkiller

ADVANCED

APHORISM
noun (<u>aa</u> fuhr ihz uhm)

....

ARABLE
adj (<u>aa</u> ruh buhl)

....

ARROGATE
verb (<u>aa</u> ruh gayt)

a short statement of a principle

The country doctor was given to such **aphorisms** as "Still waters run deep."

synonyms: adage, proverb

• •

suitable for cultivation

The overpopulated country desperately needed more **arable** land.

synonyms: farmable, fertile

• •

claim without justification; to claim for oneself without right

Lynn watched in astonishment as her boss **arrogated** the credit for her brilliant work on the project.

synonyms: take, presume, appropriate

ADVANCED

ASKANCE
adv (uh <u>skaans</u>)

· ·

ATAVISTIC
adj (aat uh <u>vihs</u> tik)

· ·

AVUNCULAR
adj (ah <u>vuhng</u> kyuh luhr)

ADVANCED

with disapproval; with a skeptical sideways glance

She looked **askance** at her son's failing report card as he mumbled that he had done all the schoolwork.

synonym: suspiciously

••

characteristic of a former era, ancient

After spending three weeks on a desert island, Roger became a survivalist with **atavistic** skills that helped him endure.

synonyms: old-fashioned, outdated

••

like an uncle in behavior, especially in kindness and warmth

The coach's **avuncular** style made him well-liked.

ADVANCED

BUCOLIC
adj (byoo <u>kahl</u> lihk)

···

CACOPHONY
noun (kuh <u>kah</u> fuh nee)

···

CALUMNY
noun (<u>kaa</u> luhm nee)

pastoral, rural

My aunt likes the hustle and bustle of the city, but my uncle prefers a more **bucolic** setting.

synonyms: rustic, country

· ·

a jarring, unpleasant noise

As I walked into the open-air market after my nap, a **cacophony** of sounds surrounded me.

synonyms: clatter, racket

· ·

a false and malicious accusation; misrepresentation

The unscrupulous politician used **calumny** to bring down his opponent in the senatorial race.

synonyms: libel, defamation, slander

CAPTIOUS
adj (<u>kaap</u> shuhs)

· ·

CELERITY
noun (seh <u>leh</u> rih tee)

· ·

CENSORIOUS
adj (sehn <u>sohr</u> ee uhs)

marked by the tendency to point out trivial faults;
intended to confuse in an argument

I resent the way he asked that **captious** question.

synonyms: critical, censorious

....

speed, haste

The celebrity ran past his fans with great **celerity**.

synonyms: swiftness, briskness

....

critical; tending to blame and condemn

Closed-minded people tend to be **censorious**
of others.

synonym: fault-finding

CHARY
adj (<u>chahr</u> ee)

. . . .

CHIMERICAL
adj (kie <u>mehr</u> ih kuhl)
(kie <u>meer</u> ih kuhl)

. . . .

COGENT
adj (<u>koh</u> juhnt)

ADVANCED

watchful, cautious; extremely shy

Mindful of the fate of the Titanic, the captain was **chary** of navigating the iceberg-filled sea.

synonyms: wary, careful

• •

fanciful; imaginary, impossible

The inventor's plans seemed **chimerical** to the conservative businessman from whom he was asking for financial support.

synonyms: illusory, unreal

• •

logically forceful; compelling, convincing

Swayed by the **cogent** argument of the defense, the jury had no choice but to acquit the defendant.

synonyms: persuasive, winning

ADVANCED

CONCOMITANT
adj (kuh <u>kahm</u> ih tuhnt)

....

CONFLAGRATION
noun (kahn fluh <u>gray</u> shuhn)

....

CONFLUENCE
noun (<u>kahn</u> floo uhns)

existing concurrently

A double-major was going to be difficult to pull off, especially since Lucy would have to juggle two papers and two exams **concomitantly**.

synonyms: coexistent, concurrent

· ·

big, destructive fire

After the **conflagration** had finally died down, the city center was nothing but a mass of blackened embers.

synonyms: blaze, inferno

· ·

the act of two things flowing together; the junction or meeting place where two things meet

At the political meeting, while planning a demonstration, there was a moving **confluence** of ideas between members.

synonyms: junction, merging

CONSANGUINEOUS
adj (kahn saang <u>gwihn</u> ee uhs)

....

CONTIGUOUS
adj (kuhn <u>tihg</u> yoo uhs)

....

CONTINENCE
noun (<u>kahn</u> tih nihns)

ADVANCED

having the same lineage or ancestry; related by blood

After having a strange feeling about our relationship for years, I found out that my best friend and I are **consanguineous**.

synonyms: kin, cognate

• •

sharing a boundary; neighboring

The two houses had **contiguous** yards so the families shared the landscaping expenses.

synonyms: bordering, adjoining

• •

self-control, self-restraint

Lucy exhibited impressive **continence** in steering clear of fattening foods, and she lost 50 pounds.

synonyms: moderation, discipline

ADVANCED

COTERIE
noun (<u>koh</u> tuh ree)

· ·

COUNTERVAIL
verb (kown tuhr <u>vayl</u>)

· ·

DECLAIM
verb (dih <u>klaym</u>)

ADVANCED

an intimate group of persons with a similar purpose

Judith invited a **coterie** of fellow stamp enthusiasts to a stamp-trading party.

synonyms: clique, set

• •

to act or react with equal force

In order to **countervail** the financial loss the school suffered after the embezzlement, the treasurer raised the price of room and board.

synonyms: counteract, compensate, offset

• •

to speak loudly and vehemently

At Thanksgiving dinner, our grandfather always **declaims** his right, as the eldest, to sit at the head of the table.

synonyms: perorate, rant, rave

ADVANCED

DEMAGOGUE
noun (<u>deh</u> muh gahg) (<u>deh</u> muh gawg)

· ·

DILUVIAL
adj (dih <u>loo</u> vee uhl)

· ·

DISCOMFIT
verb (dihs <u>kuhm</u> <u>fiht</u>)

ADVANCED

leader, rabble-rouser, usually using appeals to emotion or prejudice

Hitler began his political career as a **demagogue**, giving fiery speeches in beer halls.

synonyms: agitator, inciter, instigator

• •

pertaining to a flood

After she left the water running in the house all day, it looked simply **diluvial**.

synonym: waterlogged

• •

to disconcert, to make one lose one's composure

The class clown enjoyed **discomfiting** her classmates whenever possible.

synonyms: embarrass, thwart the plans of

ADVANCED

DISSIDENT
adj (<u>dihs</u> ih duhnt)

· ·

DOCTRINAIRE
adj (dahk truh <u>nayr</u>)

· ·

EFFLUVIA
noun (ih <u>floo</u> vee uh)

disagreeing with an established religious or
political system

The **dissident** had been living abroad and
writing his criticism of the government from an
undisclosed location.

synonym: heretical

....

rigidly devoted to theories without regard for
practicality; dogmatic

The professor's manner of teaching was
considered **doctrinaire** for such a liberal school.

synonyms: inflexible, dictatorial

....

waste; odorous fumes given off by waste

He took out the garbage at 3 A.M. because the
effluvia had begun wafting into the bedroom.

synonyms: odor, stench

ADVANCED

EPOCHAL
adj (ehp uh kuhl) (ehp ahk uhl)

....

EPONYMOUS
adj (ih pahn uh muhs)

....

EQUIVOCATE
verb (ih kwihv uh kayt)

ADVANCED

momentous, highly significant

The Supreme Court's **epochal** decision will no doubt affect generations to come.

synonyms: unparalleled, notable

• •

giving one's name to a place, book, restaurant

Macbeth was the **eponymous** protagonist of Shakespeare's play.

synonym: named after

• •

to avoid committing oneself in what one says, to be deliberately unclear

Not wanting to implicate himself in the crime, the suspect **equivocated** for hours.

synonyms: lie, mislead

ADVANCED

ERSATZ
adj (uhr <u>sahtz</u>)

....

EXCORIATE
verb (ehk <u>skohr</u> ee ayt)

....

EXTIRPATE
verb (<u>ehk</u> stuhr payt)

being an artificial and inferior substitute or imitation

The **ersatz** strawberry shortcake tasted more like plastic than like real cake.

synonyms: fake, counterfeit

· ·

to censure scathingly; to express strong disapproval of

The three-page letter to the editor **excoriated** the publication for printing the rumor without verifying the source.

synonym: denounce

· ·

to root out, eradicate, literally or figuratively; to destroy wholly

The terrorist cells were **extirpated** after many years of investigation.

synonym: wipe out

ADVANCED

EXTRAPOLATION
verb (ihk <u>strap</u> uh lay shuhn)

....

EXTRINSIC
adj (ihk <u>strihn</u> sihk) (ihk <u>strihn</u> zihk)

....

EXTRUDE
verb (ihk <u>strood</u>)

ADVANCED

using known data and information to determine what will happen in the future, prediction

Through the process of **extrapolation**, we were able to determine which mutual funds to invest in.

synonyms: projection, forecast

••

external, unessential; originating from the outside

"Though they are interesting to note," the meeting manager claimed, "those facts are **extrinsic** to the matter under discussion."

synonyms: extraneous, foreign

••

to form or shape something by pushing it out, to force out, especially through a small opening

We watched in awe as the volcano **extruded** molten lava.

synonym: squeeze out

ADVANCED

FALLACIOUS
adj (fuh <u>lay</u> shuhs)

· ·

FEBRILE
adj (<u>fehb</u> ruhl) (<u>fee</u> bruhl)

· ·

FECKLESS
adj (<u>fehk</u> lihs)

ADVANCED

tending to deceive or mislead; based on a fallacy

The **fallacious** statement "the Earth is flat" misled people for many years.

synonyms: false, erroneous

....

feverish, marked by intense emotion or activity

Awaiting the mysterious announcement, there was a **febrile** excitement in the crowd.

synonyms: agitated, flushed

....

ineffective, worthless

Anja took on the responsibility of caring for her aged mother, realizing that her **feckless** sister was not up to the task.

synonym: incompetent

ADVANCED

FICTIVE
adj (<u>fihk</u> tihv)

....

FILIBUSTER
verb (<u>fihl</u> ih buhs tuhr)

....

FORTUITOUS
adj (fohr <u>too</u> ih tuhs)

fictional, relating to imaginative creation

She found she was more productive when writing **fictive** stories rather than autobiography.

synonym: not genuine

• •

to use obstructionist tactics, especially prolonged speech making, in order to delay something

The congressman read names from the phonebook in an attempt to **filibuster** a pending bill.

synonym: stall

• •

by chance, especially by favorable chance

After a **fortuitous** run-in with an agent, Roxy won a recording contract.

synonym: accidental

ADVANCED

FRENETIC
adj (freh <u>neht</u> ihk)

....

FULSOME
adj (<u>fool</u> suhm)

....

GALVANIZE
verb (<u>gaal</u> vuh niez)

frantic, frenzied

The employee's **frenetic** schedule left him little time to socialize.

synonym: feverish

· ·

abundant; flattering in an insincere way

The king's servant showered him with **fulsome** compliments in hopes of currying favor.

synonym: too complimentary

· ·

to shock; to arouse awareness

The closing down of another homeless shelter **galvanized** the activist group into taking political action.

synonym: vitalize, energize

GAMELY
adj (<u>gaym</u> lee)

· ·

GAUCHE
adj (gohsh)

· ·

GRANDILOQUENCE
noun (graan <u>dihl</u> uh kwuhns)

spiritedly, bravely

The park ranger **gamely** navigated the trail up the steepest face of the mountain.

synonym: excitedly

••

lacking social refinement

Snapping one's fingers to get the waiter's attention is considered **gauche**.

synonyms: tactless, simple

••

pompous talk; fancy but meaningless language

The headmistress was notorious for her **grandiloquence** at the lectern and her ostentatious clothes.

synonyms: bravado, pretension

GREGARIOUS
adj (greh <u>gaar</u> ee uhs)

··

HARANGUE
verb (huh <u>raang</u>)

··

HEGEMONY
noun (hih <u>jeh</u> muh nee)

outgoing, sociable

Unlike her introverted friends, Susan was very **gregarious**.

synonyms: convivial, friendly

· ·

to give a long speech

Maria's parents **harangued** her when she told them she'd spent her money on magic beans.

synonyms: lecture, reprimand

· ·

the domination of one state or group over its allies

When Germany claimed **hegemony** over Russia, Stalin was outraged.

synonyms: power, authority

ADVANCED

HERETICAL
adj (huh <u>reh</u> tih kuhl)

· ·

HISTRIONICS
noun (hihs tree <u>ahn</u> ihks)

· ·

HUBRIS
noun (<u>hyoo</u> brihs)

departing from accepted beliefs or standards, oppositional

At the onset of the Inquisition, the **heretical** priest was forced to flee the country.

synonym: unorthodox

••

deliberate display of emotion for effect; exaggerated behavior calculated for effect

With such **histrionics,** she should really consider becoming an actress.

synonyms: melodrama, theatrics

••

excessive pride or self-confidence

Nathan's **hubris** spurred him to do things that many considered insensitive.

sysnonyms: presumption, arrogance

HUSBAND
verb (<u>huhz</u> buhnd)

· ·

IGNOBLE
adj (ihg <u>noh</u> buhl)

· ·

ILLUSORY
adj (ih <u>loo</u> suhr ee) (ih <u>loos</u> ree)

to manage economically; to use sparingly

The cyclist paced herself at the start of the race, knowing that if she **husbanded** her resources she'd have the strength to break out of the pack later on.

synonym: conserve

• •

having low moral standards, not noble in character; mean

The photographer was paid a princely sum for the picture of the self-proclaimed ethicist in the **ignoble** act of pick-pocketing.

synonyms: lowly, vulgar

• •

producing illusion, deceptive

The desert explorer was devastated to discover that the lake he thought he had seen was in fact **illusory**.

synonyms: false, imaginary

IMPERIOUS
adj (ihm <u>pihr</u> ee uhs)

. . . .

IMPERTURBABLE
adj (<u>ihm</u> puhr <u>tuhr</u> buh buhl)

. . . .

IMPLACABLE
adj (ihm <u>play</u> kuh buhl)
(ihm <u>plaa</u> kuh buhl)

ADVANCED

commanding, domineering; urgent

Though the king had been a kind leader, his daughter was **imperious** and demanding during her rule.

synonym: authoritarian

••

unshakably calm and steady

No matter how disruptive the children became, the babysitter remained **imperturbable**.

synonyms: cool, unflappable

••

inflexible; not capable of being changed or pacified

The **implacable** teasing was hard for the child to take.

synonyms: merciless, relentless

ADVANCED

IMPORTUNATE
adj (ihm <u>pohr</u> chuh niht)

· ·

IMPRECATION
noun (ihm prih <u>kay</u> shuhn)

· ·

IMPUTE
verb (ihm <u>pyoot</u>)

troublesomely urgent; extremely persistent in request or demand

Her **importunate** appeal for a job caused me to grant her an interview.

synonyms: insistent, obstinate

. . . .

a curse

Spouting violent **imprecations,** Hank searched for the person who had vandalized his truck.

synonym: damnation

. . . .

to lay the responsibility or blame for, often unjustly

It seemed unfair to **impute** the accident on me, especially since they were the ones who ran the red light.

synonyms: ascribe, attribute, pin on

INCARNADINE
adj (ihn <u>kaar</u> nuh dien)
(ihn <u>kaar</u> nuh dihn)

· ·

INCHOATE
adj (ihn <u>koh</u> iht)

· ·

INSENSATE
adj (ihn <u>sehn</u> sayt) (ihn <u>sehn</u> siht)

ADVANCED

red, especially blood red

The **incarnadine** lipstick she wore made her look much older than she was.

· ·

being only partly in existence; imperfectly formed

For every page of the crisp writing that made it into the final book, Jessie has 10 pages of **inchoate** rambling that made up the first draft.

synonyms: formless, undefined

· ·

lacking sensibility and understanding, foolish

The shock of the accident left him **insensate**, but after some time, the numbness subsided and he was able to tell the officer what had happened.

synonyms: unfeeling, callous

ADVANCED

INSUPERABLE
adj (ihn <u>soo</u> puhr uh buhl)

....

INTERLOCUTOR
noun (ihn tuhr <u>lahk</u> yuh tuhr)

....

INTERNECINE
adj (ihn tuhr <u>nehs</u> een)

incapable of being surmounted or overcome

Insuperable as though our problems may seem, I'm confident we'll come out ahead.

synonym: unconquerable

•••

ones who takes part in conversation

Though always the **interlocutor,** the professor actually preferred that his students guide the class discussion.

•••

equally devastating to both sides

Though it looked as though there was a victor, the **internecine** battle benefited no one.

synonym: mutually destructive

ADVANCED

INTERREGNUM
noun (ihn tuhr <u>rehg</u> nuhm)

••

INVETERATE
adj (ihn <u>veht</u> uhr iht)

••

IRASCIBLE
adj (ih <u>raas</u> uh buhl)

ADVANCED

a temporary halting of the usual operations of government or control

The new king began his reign by restoring order that the lawless **interregnum** had destroyed.

synonyms: hiatus, interruption

· ·

firmly established, especially with respect to a habit or attitude

An **inveterate** risk-taker, Lori tried her luck at bungee-jumping.

synonyms: habitual, chronic

· ·

easily angered, hot-tempered

One of the most **irascible** barbarians of all time, Attila the Hun ravaged much of Europe during his time.

synonyms: irritable, crabby

JOCULAR
adj (<u>jahk</u> yuh luhr)

• •

JUNTA
noun (<u>hoon</u> tuh) (<u>juhn</u> tuh)

• •

LARGESS
noun (laar <u>jehs</u>)

playful, humorous

The **jocular** old man entertained his grandchildren for hours.

synonyms: comical, amusing

....

a small governing body, especially after a revolutionary seizure of power

Only one member of the **junta** was satisfactory enough to be elected once the new government was established.

synonym: council

....

generous giving (as of money) to others who may seem inferior

She'd always relied on her parent's **largess**, but after graduation, she had to get a job.

ADVANCED

LEXICON
noun (<u>lehk</u> sih kahn)

....

LICENTIOUS
adj (lih <u>sehn</u> shuhs)

....

LOQUACIOUS
adj (loh <u>kway</u> shuhs)

a dictionary; a stock of terms pertaining to a particular subject or vocabulary

The author coined the term Gen-X, which has since entered the **lexicon.**

synonyms: dictionary, vocabulary

· ·

immoral; unrestrained by society

Religious citizens were outraged by the **licentious** exploits of the free-spirited artists living in town.

synonyms: wanton, lewd

· ·

talkative

She was naturally **loquacious,** which was always a challenge when she was in a library or movie theater.

synonym: chatty

MACABRE
adj (muh <u>kaa</u> bruh) (muh <u>kaa</u> buhr)

·······································

MACROCOSM
noun (<u>maak</u> roh cahz uhm)

·······································

MALAPROPISM
noun (<u>maal</u> uh prahp ihz uhm)

having death as a subject; dwelling on the gruesome

Martin enjoyed **macabre** tales about werewolves and vampires.

synonyms: ghastly, grim

. . . .

the whole universe; a large-scale reflection of a part of the great world

Some scientists focus on a particular aspect of space, while others study the entire **macrocosm** and how its parts relate to one another.

synonym: cosmos

. . . .

the accidental, often comical, use of a word which resembles the one intended, but has a different, often contradictory meaning

She meant to say "public broadcasting" but instead it came out a **malapropism**: "public boredcasting."

synonym: misstatement

MALFEASANCE
noun (maal <u>fee</u> zuhns)

....

MAWKISH
adj (<u>maw</u> kihsh)

....

MELLIFLUOUS
adj (muh <u>lihf</u> loo uhs)

wrongdoing or misconduct, especially by a
public official

Not only was the deputy's **malfeasance**
humiliating, it also spelled the end of his career.

synonyms: corruption, fraud

· ·

sickeningly sentimental

The poet hoped to charm his girlfriend with his
flowery poem, but its **mawkish** tone sickened
her instead.

synonym: maudlin

· ·

having a smooth, rich flow

She was so talented that her **mellifluous** flute
playing transported me to another world.

synonym: melodious

ADVANCED

MILIEU
noun (mihl <u>yoo</u>)

. . . .

MORDANT
adj (<u>mohr</u> dnt)

. . . .

MORES
noun (<u>mawr</u> ayz)

the physical or social setting in which something occurs or develops, environment

The **milieu** at the club wasn't one I was comfortable with, so I left right away.

synonym: background

• •

biting and caustic in manner and style

Roald Dahl's stories are **mordant** alternatives to bland kids' stories.

synonyms: scathing, hurtful

• •

fixed customs or manners; moral attitudes

In keeping with the **mores** of ancient Roman society, Nero held a celebration every weekend.

synonyms: conventions, practices

MOTE
noun (moht)

....

NEONATE
noun (<u>nee</u> uh nayt)

....

NOMENCLATURE
noun (<u>noh</u> muhn klay chuhr)

a small particle, speck

Monica's eye watered, irritated by a **mote** of dust.

synonyms: bit, shred

···

a newborn child

The **neonate** was born prematurely so she's still in the hospital.

synonyms: baby, infant

···

a system of scientific names

In botany class, we learned the **nomenclature** used to identify different species of roses.

synonyms: classification, codification

ADVANCED

OBDURATE
adj (<u>ahb</u> duhr uht)

··

OBFUSCATE
verb (<u>ahb</u> fyoo skayt)

··

OPPROBRIOUS
adj (uh <u>proh</u> bree uhs)

stubbornly persistent, resistant to persuasion

The president was **obdurate** on the matter, and no amount of public protest could change his mind.

synonyms: inflexible, inexorable, adamant

· ·

to confuse, make obscure

Benny always **obfuscates** the discussion by bringing in irrelevant facts.

synonyms: shadow, complicate

· ·

disgraceful, shameful

She wrote an **opprobrious** editorial in the newspaper about the critic who tore her new play to shreds.

synonym: scornful

ADVANCED

OSSIFY
verb (<u>ah</u> sih fie)

....

PALIMPSEST
noun (<u>pahl</u> ihmp sehst)

....

PANEGYRIC
noun (paan uh <u>geer</u> ihk)

to change into bone; to become hardened or set in a rigidly conventional pattern

The forensics expert ascertained the body's age based on the degree to which the facial structure had **ossified.**

••

an object or place having diverse layers or aspects beneath the surface

Paper was very expensive, so the practice was to write over previous words, creating a **palimpsest** of writing.

••

elaborate praise; formal hymn of praise

The director's **panegyric** for the donor who kept his charity going was heart-warming.

synonyms: compliment, homage

PECULATE
verb (<u>pehk</u> yuh layt)

. . . .

PECUNIARY
adj (pih <u>kyoon</u> nee <u>ehr</u> ee)

. . . .

PELLUCID
adj (peh <u>loo</u> sihd)

ADVANCED

to embezzle

These days in the news, we read more and more about workers **peculating** the system.

synonym: misappropriate

• •

relating to money

Michelle's official title was office manager, but she ended up taking on a lot of **pecuniary** responsibilities such as payroll duties.

synonyms: fiscal, financial

• •

transparently clear in style or meaning, easy to understand

Though she thought she could hide her ulterior motives, they were **pellucid** to everyone else.

synonym: apparent

ADVANCED

PENURY
noun (<u>pehn</u> yuh ree)

....

PEREGRINATE
verb (<u>pehr</u> ih gruh nayt)

....

PHILOLOGY
noun (fih <u>lahl</u> uh jee)

ADVANCED

an oppressive lack of resources (as money), severe poverty

Once a famous actor, he eventually died in **penury** and anonymity.

synonyms: destitution, impoverishment

· ·

to travel on foot

It has always been a dream of mine to **peregrinate** from one side of Europe to the other with nothing but a backpack.

synonyms: walk, traverse

· ·

the study of ancient texts and languages

Philology was the predecessor to modern-day linguistics.

ADVANCED

POLYGLOT
noun (<u>pah</u> lee glaht)

. . . .

POTENTATE
noun (<u>poh</u> tehn tayt)

. . . .

PRESTIDIGITATION
noun (<u>prehs</u> tih <u>dihj</u> ih <u>tay</u> shuhn)

ADVANCED

a speaker of many languages

Ling's extensive travels have helped her to become a true **polyglot**.

· ·

a ruler; one who wields great power

Alex was much kinder before he assumed the role of **potentate**.

synonyms: leader, dominator

· ·

a cleverly executed trick or deception; sleight of hand

My hunch was that he won the contest not so much as a result of real talent, but rather through **prestidigitation**.

ADVANCED

PROMULGATE
verb (<u>prah</u> muhl gayt)

• •

PROSCRIBE
verb (proh <u>skrieb</u>)

• •

PUISSANT
adj (<u>pwih</u> sihnt) (<u>pyoo</u> sihnt)

to make known by open declaration, proclaim

The publicist **promulgated** the idea that the celebrity had indeed gotten married.

synonyms: announce, broadcast

· ·

to condemn or forbid as harmful or unlawful

Consumption of alcohol was **proscribed** in the country's constitution, but the ban was eventually lifted.

synonyms: prohibit, ban

· ·

powerful

His memoir was full of descriptions of **puissant** military heroics, but most were exaggerations or outright lies.

synonyms: strong, mighty

ADVANCED

PUNCTILIOUS
adj (puhngk <u>tihl</u> ee uhs)

· ·

RAPACIOUS
adj (ruh <u>pay</u> shuhs)

· ·

RECAPITULATE
verb (<u>ree</u> kuh <u>pihch</u> yoo layt)

ADVANCED

concerned with precise details about codes or conventions

The **punctilious** student never made spelling errors on her essays.

synonyms: precise, scrupulous, meticulous

• •

taking by force; driven by greed

Sea otters are so **rapacious** that they consume 10 times their body weight in food every day.

synonyms: ravenous, voracious

• •

to review by a brief summary

After the long-winded president had finished his speech, his assistant **recapitulated** for the press the points he had made.

synonyms: synopsize, condense, digest

ADVANCED

RECIDIVISM
noun (rih <u>sihd</u> uh vih zihm)

....

ROSTRUM
noun (<u>rahs</u> truhm)

....

SANCTIMONIOUS
adj (<u>saangk</u> tih <u>moh</u> nee uhs)

a tendency to relapse into a previous behavior, especially criminal behavior

According to statistics, the **recidivism** rate for criminals is quite high.

synonyms: return, backslide, relapse

• •

an elevated platform for public speaking

Though she was terrified, the new member of the debate club approached the **rostrum** with poise.

synonyms: stage, podium

• •

hypocritically devout; acting morally superior to another

The **sanctimonious** columnist turned out to have been hiding a gambling problem that cost his family everything.

synonyms: holier-than-thou, self-righteous

SATURNINE
adj (<u>saat</u> uhr nien)

· ·

SEDITION
noun (seh <u>dih</u> shuhn)

· ·

SEMINAL
adj (<u>seh</u> muhn uhl)

ADVANCED

cold and steady in mood, gloomy; slow to act

Her **saturnine** expression every day made her hard to be around.

synonyms: sullen, bitter

••

behavior that promotes rebellion or civil disorder against the state

Li was arrested for **sedition** after he gave a fiery speech in the main square.

synonyms: insurrection, conspiracy

••

influential in an original way, providing a basis for further development; creative

The scientist's discovery proved to be **seminal** in the area of quantum physics.

synonyms: original, generative

ADVANCED

SERAPHIC
adj (seh <u>rah</u> fihk)

∙∙

SINECURE
noun (<u>sien</u> ih kyoor)

∙∙

SOBRIQUET
noun (<u>soh</u> brih <u>kay</u>) (<u>soh</u> brih <u>keht</u>)

ADVANCED

angelic, sweet

Selena's **seraphic** appearance belied her nasty, bitter personality.

synonyms: heavenly, cherubic

· ·

a well-paying job or office that requires little or no work

The corrupt mayor made sure to set up all his relatives in **sinecures** within the administration.

· ·

a nickname

One of former president Ronald Reagan's **sobriquets** was *The Gipper*.

synonyms: alias, pseudonym

ADVANCED

SOLICITOUS
adj (suh <u>lih</u> sih tuhs)

· ·

SPECIOUS
adj (<u>spee</u> shuhs)

· ·

STASIS
noun (<u>stay</u> sihs)

ADVANCED

anxious, concerned; full of desire, eager

Overjoyed to see the pop idol in her very presence, the **solicitous** store owner stood ready to serve.

synonyms: considerate, careful

....

having the ring of truth but actually being untrue; deceptively attractive

After I followed up with some research on the matter, I realized that the charismatic politician's argument had been **specious**.

synonyms: misleading, untrue, captious

....

a state of static balance or equilibrium; stagnation

The rusty, ivy-covered World War II tank had obviously been in **stasis** for years.

synonyms: inertia, standstill

ADVANCED

STRATIFY
verb (<u>straa</u> tuh fie)

. . . .

STRIDENT
adj (<u>strie</u> dehnt)

. . . .

SUPERFLUOUS
adj (soo <u>puhr</u> floo <u>uhs</u>)

ADVANCED

to arrange or divide into layers

Schliemann **stratified** the numerous layers of Troy, an archeological dig that remains legendary.

synonyms: grade, separate

. . . .

loud, harsh, unpleasantly noisy

The traveler's **strident** manner annoyed the flight attendant, but she managed to keep her cool.

synonyms: grating, shrill, discordant

. . . .

extra, more than necessary

The extra recommendations Jake included in his application were **superfluous,** as only one was required.

synonyms: excess, surplus

ADVANCED

SUPPLANT
verb (suh <u>plaant</u>)

··

SYBARITE
noun (<u>sih</u> buh riet)

··

TANTAMOUNT
adj (<u>taan</u> tuh mownt)

to replace (another) by force, to take the place of

The overthrow of the government meant a new leader to **supplant** the tyrannical former one.

synonyms: displace, supersede

• •

a person devoted to pleasure and luxury

A confirmed **sybarite**, the nobleman fainted at the thought of having to leave his palace and live in a small cottage.

synonym: epicure

• •

equal in value or effect

If she didn't get concert tickets to see her favorite band, it would be **tantamount** to a tragedy.

synonyms: parallel, synonymous, equivalent

ADVANCED

TAUTOLOGICAL
adj (<u>tawt</u> uh <u>lah</u> jih kuhl)

....

TEMERITY
noun (<u>teh</u> mehr ih tee)

....

TEMPORAL
adj (<u>tehmp</u> ore uhl)

having to do with needless repetition, redundancy

I know he was only trying to clarify things, but his **tautological** statements confused me even more.

synonyms: verbose, wordy

. . . .

unreasonable or foolhardy disregard for danger, recklessness

I offered her a ride since it was late at night, but she had the **temerity** to say she'd rather walk.

synonyms: boldness, audacity

. . . .

having to do with time

The story lacked a sense of the **temporal,** so we couldn't figure out if the events took place in one evening or over the course of a year.

ADVANCED

TENUOUS
adj (<u>tehn</u> yoo uhs)

....

TITULAR
adj (<u>tihch</u> yoo luhr)

....

TOADY
noun (<u>toh</u> dee)

having little substance or strength; flimsy, weak

Francine's already **tenuous** connection to her cousins was broken when they moved away and left no forwarding address.

synonyms: thin, shaky

• •

existing in title only; having a title without the functions or responsibilities

Margaret is the **titular** head of the company.

synonyms: honorary, named

• •

one who flatters in the hope of gaining favors

The king was surrounded by **toadies** who rushed to agree with whatever outrageous thing he said.

synonyms: sycophant, parasite

ADVANCED

TORTUOUS
adj (<u>tohr</u> choo uhs)

· ·

TRUCULENT
adj (<u>truhk</u> yuh lehnt)

· ·

TURGID
adj (<u>tuhr</u> jihd)

having many twists and turns; highly complex

To reach the remote inn, the travelers had to negotiate a **tortuous** path.

synonyms: winding, circuitous

....

disposed to fight, belligerent

The bully was initially **truculent** but eventually stopped picking fights at the least provocation.

synonyms: antagonistic, combative

....

swollen as from a fluid, bloated

In the process of osmosis, water passes through the walls of **turgid** cells, ensuring that they never contain too much water.

synonyms: distended, protuberant, tumescent

TUTELAGE
noun (<u>toot</u> uh lihj)

....

USURY
noun (<u>yoo</u> zuh ree)

....

VARIEGATED
adj (<u>vaar</u> ee uh <u>gayt</u> ehd)

guardianship, guidance

Under the **tutelage** of her older sister, the young orphan was able to persevere.

synonym: supervision

• •

the practice of lending money at exorbitant rates

The moneylender was convicted of **usury** when it was discovered that he charged 50 percent interest on all his loans.

synonyms: loan-sharking, interest

• •

varied; marked with different colors

The **variegated** foliage of the jungle allows it to support thousands of animal species.

synonym: diversified

ADVANCED

VERNAL
adj (<u>vuhr</u> nuhl)

· ·

VIM
noun (vihm)

· ·

VITUPERATE
verb (vie <u>too</u> puhr ayt)

related to spring; fresh

Bea basked in the balmy **vernal** breezes, happy that winter was coming to an end.

synonyms: springlike, youthful

•••

vitality and energy

The **vim** with which she worked so early in the day explained why she was so productive.

synonyms: power, force

•••

to abuse verbally, berate

Vituperating someone is never a constructive way to effect change.

synonyms: scold, reproach, castigate

ADVANCED

VOCIFEROUS
adj (voh <u>sih</u> fuhr uhs)

∙∙∙

VOLUBLE
adj (<u>vahl</u> yuh buhl)

∙∙∙

WAX
verb (waaks)

ADVANCED

loud, noisy

Amid the **vociferous** protests of the members of parliament, the prime minister continued his speech.

synonyms: vocal, boisterous

• •

talkative, speaking easily, glib

The **voluble** man and his reserved wife proved the old saying that opposites attract.

synonyms: loquacious, verbose

• •

to increase gradually; to begin to be

The moon was **waxing,** and would soon be full.

synonyms: enlarge, expand

ADVANCED

ZENITH
noun (<u>zee</u> nihth)

....

ZEPHYR
noun (<u>zeh</u> fuhr)

....

the point of culmination; peak

The diva considered her appearance at the Metropolitan Opera to be the **zenith** of her career.

synonyms: acme, pinnacle

•••

a gentle breeze; something airy or unsubstantial

The **zephyr** from the ocean made the intense heat on the beach bearable for the sunbathers.

synonyms: breath, draft

•••

ADVANCED

SAT ROOT LIST

A, AN—not, without
AB, A—from, away, apart
AC, ACR—sharp, sour
AD, A—to, towards
ALI, ALTR—another
AM, AMI—love
AMBI, AMPHI—both
AMBL, AMBUL—walk
ANIM—mind, spirit, breath
ANN, ENN—year
ANTE, ANT—before
ANTHROP—human
ANTI, ANT—against, opposite
AUD—hear
AUTO—self
BELLI, BELL—war
BENE, BEN—good
BI—two
BIBLIO—book
BIO—life
BURS—money, purse
CAD, CAS, CID—happen, fall
CAP, CIP—head
CARN—flesh

CAP, CAPT, CEPT, CIP—take, hold, seize
CED, CESS—yield, go
CHROM—color
CHRON—time
CIDE—murder
CIRCUM—around
CLIN, CLIV—slope
CLUD, CLUS, CLAUS, CLOIS—shut, close
CO, COM, CON—with, together
COGN, GNO—know
CONTRA—against
CORP—body
COSMO, COSM—world
CRAC, CRAT—rule, power
CRED—trust, believe
CRESC, CRET—grow
CULP—blame, fault
CURR, CURS—run
DE—down, out, apart
DEC—ten, tenth
DEMO, DEM—people

DI, DIURN—day

DIA—across

DIC, DICT—speak

DIS, DIF, DI—not, apart, away

DOC, DOCT—teach

DOL—pain

DUC, DUCT—lead

EGO—self

EN, EM—in, into

ERR—wander

EU—well, good

EX, E—out, out of

FAC, FIC, FECT, FY, FEA—
    make, do

FAL, FALS—deceive

FERV—boil

FID—faith, trust

FLU, FLUX—flow

FORE—before

FRAG, FRAC—break

FUS—pour

GEN—birth, class, kin

GRAD, GRESS—step

GRAPH, GRAM—writing

GRAT—pleasing

GRAV, GRIEV—heavy

GREG—crowd, flock

HABIT, HIBIT—have, hold

HAP—by chance

HELIO, HELI—sun

HETERO—other

HOL—whole

HOMO—same

HOMO—man

HYDR—water

HYPER—too much, excess

HYPO—too little, under

IN, IG, IL, IM, IR—not

IN, IL, IM, IR—in, on, into

INTER—between, among

INTRA, INTR—within

IT, ITER—between, among

JECT, JET—throw

JOUR—day

JUD—judge

JUNCT, JUG—join

JUR—swear, law

LAT—side

LAV, LAU, LU—wash

LEG, LEC, LEX—read, speak

LEV—light

LIBER—free

LIG, LECT—choose, gather

LIG, LI, LY—bind

LING, LANG—tongue

LITER—letter

LITH—stone

LOQU, LOC, LOG—speech,
    thought

LUC, LUM—light

LUD, LUS—play

MACRO—great

MAG, MAJ, MAS, MAX—great

MAL—bad

MAN—hand

MAR—sea

MATER, MATR—mother

MEDI—middle

MEGA—great

MEM, MEN—remember

METER, METR, MENS—
    measure

MICRO—small

MIS—wrong, bad, hate

MIT, MISS—send

MOLL—soft

MON, MONIT—warn

MONO—one

MOR—custom, manner

MOR, MORT—dead

MORPH—shape

MOV, MOT, MOB, MOM—move

MUT—change

NAT, NASC—born

NAU, NAV—ship, sailor

NEG—not, deny

NEO—new

NIHIL—none, nothing

NOM, NYM—name

NOX, NIC, NEC, NOC—harm

NOV—new

NUMER—number

OB—against

OMNI—all

ONER—burden

OPER—work

PAC—peace

PALP—feel

PAN—all

PATER, PATR—father

PATH, PASS—feel, suffer

PEC—money

PED, POD—foot

PEL, PULS—drive

PEN—almost

PEND, PENS—hang

PER—through, by, for,
    throughout

PER—against, destruction

PERI—around

PET—seek, go towards

PHIL—love

PHOB—fear

PHON—sound

PLAC—calm, please

PON, POS—put, place

PORT—carry

POT—drink

POT—power

PRE—before

PRIM, PRI—first

PRO—ahead, forth

PROTO—first

PROX, PROP—near

SAT ROOT LIST

PSEUDO—false

PYR—fire

QUAD, QUAR, QUAT—four

QUES, QUER, QUIS, QUIR—question

QUIE—quiet

QUINT, QUIN—five

RADI, RAMI—branch

RECT, REG—straight, rule

REG—king, rule

RETRO—backward

RID, RIS—laugh

ROG—ask

RUD—rough, crude

RUPT—break

SACR, SANCT—holy

SCRIB, SCRIPT, SCRIV—write

SE—apart, away

SEC, SECT, SEG—cut

SED, SID—sit

SEM—seed, sow

SEN—old

SENT, SENS—feel, think

SEQU, SECU—follow

SIM, SEM—similar, same

SIGN—mark, sign

SIN—curve

SOL—sun

SOL—alone

SOMN—sleep

SON—sound

SOPH—wisdom

SPEC, SPIC—see, look

SPER—hope

SPERS, SPAR—scatter

SPIR—breathe

STRICT, STRING—bind

STRUCT, STRU—build

SUB—under

SUMM—highest

SUPER, SUR—above

SURGE, SURRECT—rise

SYN, SYM—together

TACIT, TIC—silent

TACT, TAG, TANG—touch

TEN, TIN, TAIN—hold, twist

TEND, TENS, TENT—stretch

TERM—end

TERR—earth, land

TEST—witness

THE—god

THERM—heat

TIM—fear, frightened

TOP—place

TORT—twist

TORP—stiff, numb

TOX—poison

TRACT—draw

TRANS—across, over, through, beyond

TREM, TREP—shake

TURB—shake

UMBR—shadow

UNI, UN—one

URB—city

VAC—empty

VAL, VAIL—value, strength

VEN, VENT—come

VER—true

VERB—word

VERT, VERS—turn

VICT, VINC—conquer

VID, VIS—see

VIL—base, mean

VIV, VIT—life

VOC, VOK, VOW—call, voice

VOL—wish

VOLV, VOLUT—turn, roll

VOR—eat

Take your SAT prep to the next level with Kaplan Premier Tutoring

Personal Attention. Convenience. Proven Results.

See the difference that one-on-one in-home tutoring can make on the SAT or the ACT. Call today for a free consultation.